BADMINTON

about the author

Margaret Varner Bloss's experience is not confined to her native Texas nor to the United States but spreads throughout the world.

She is the only person ever to represent the United States in international competition in three racket sports: tennis (Wightman Cup), squash rackets (Wolfe-Noel Cup), and badminton (Uber Cup).

In addition to being the National Junior Girls' Doubles Champion, Mrs. Bloss was a member of the United States Wightman Cup Team in 1961 and 1962 and coach and/or captain of that team 1963-66. She holds U.S., England, and world titles in badminton and squash rackets: world champion 1955 and 1956; U.S. singles champion, 1956; mixed doubles champion, 1960; four years as world invitation ladies doubles champion, Glasgow, Scotland, and many more records in badminton, and national ladies singles champion 1960 through 1963 in squash rackets; finalist in U.S. ladies doubles championship in 1961, and member of the U.S. Wolfe-Noel Team in 1959 and 1963 and of the Philadelphia Howe Cup Team 1959-63. In 1969 she was captain of the U.S. Uber Cup team.

Mrs. Bloss is also known for her books and articles on badminton and other sports. She has conducted workshops and clinics on tennis and badminton at Wellesley College, and the universities of Maryland, Delaware, Utah, and Texas Woman's. She has traveled throughout the world giving talks, exhibitions and clinics.

Mrs. Bloss lives with her two young children in El Paso, Texas, where she continues her interest in sports and with Margaret Osborne duPont breeds and raises racehorses.

BADMINTON
Fourth Edition

Physical Education Activities Series

MARGARET VARNER BLOSS
Former World Badminton Champion

Cover photo courtesy of The Travelers Insurance Companies

ωcb
Wm. C. Brown Company Publishers
Dubuque, Iowa

Consulting Editors

Physical Education
Aileene Lockhart
Texas Woman's University

Parks and Recreation
David Gray
California State University, Long Beach

Health
Robert Kaplan
The Ohio State University

**Physical Education Activities
Evaluation Materials Editor**

Jane A. Mott
Texas Woman's University

Copyright © 1971, 1975, 1980 by Wm. C. Brown Company Publishers

Library of Congress Catalog Card Number: 79-93336

ISBN 0-697-07096-4

Printed in the United States of America

contents

preface

Although this book is designed primarily for college physical education classes, the information is clearly suitable for and useful to backyard, club or tournament players. Beginning students can grasp essentials by reason of the text modified for easy assimilation enabling them to learn readily step by step. Advanced students can refresh forgotten procedures by skimming through added headings and topic sentences in shortened paragraphs or by merely referring to the table of contents.

Enhancing the easy text is the precision of the new drawings that have replaced the photographs of earlier editions. The decision to replace photographs with drawings was made with some trepidation at first, but all doubts were erased once the first trial drawing was submitted. The artist has made it possible for badminton students to learn precisely the delicate, sometimes intricate muscle changes that occur in various arm movements. In one sense, the drawings are more realistic than the photographs were because of this very precision.

The combination of easy text, precise illustrations and updated material throughout will enable badminton enthusiasts to increase their enjoyment of the game.

acknowledgments

Thanks are due the United States Badminton Association for supplying constructive suggestions and relevant material promptly and willingly. Artists Jerry Knotts and Ignacio Garcia, Jr. of El Paso are responsible for the finely detailed illustrations. Bea Bragg and Lyn Ruggiero, of B-R and Associates, also of El Paso, assisted in editorial matters.

what badminton
is like

1

HISTORICAL NOTES

Badminton, a game which gets its name from an English estate, is played with
rackets and shuttlecocks on a court divided by a net. It appears to have been
played in India and England in the mid and late nineteenth century. However,
since that time, the game has enjoyed considerable popularity in many countries. Always very well liked in the British Isles, badminton is also considered
virtually the national sport in India, Malaysia, Indonesia and Thailand. Denmark, Sweden and West Germany lead the European countries in their interest.
The game spread to Canada and the United States where national organizations
similar to those of other countries were formed. The number of clubs in the
U.S. is not comparable, however, to the number found in the aforementioned
countries.

BADMINTON FOR FITNESS AND RECREATION

As leisure time increases, badminton will no doubt play an important role in
the fitness and recreational programs so vital to the American citizen. It can
be played by men, women, and children of all ages with a minimum of expense
and effort. The game itself is stimulating mentally and physically, and it com-
bines the values of individual and team sports. The fact that it can be learned
easily makes it enjoyable from the outset. Basic techniques are easy to learn, yet
much practice and concentration are required to perfect the skills needed for
becoming a really good badminton player.

THE GAME

Badminton can be played indoors or outdoors, under artificial or natural lighting. There may be two players on a side (the four-handed or doubles game) or
one player on a side (the two-handed or singles game). The shuttlecock does
not bounce; therefore it is played in the air, making for an exceptionally fast
game requiring quick reflexes and superb conditioning. There is a wide variety

1

of strokes in the game ranging from powerfully hit smashes to very delicately played dropshots.

Badminton is a fun game because it is easy to play—the shuttlecock can be hit back and forth (rallies) even when the players possess a minimum of skill. Within a week or two after the beginning of a class, rallies and scoring can take place. There are very few sports in which it is possible to get the feeling of having become an "instant player." However, do not assume that perfection of strokes and tournament caliber of play is by any means less difficult in badminton than in other sports.

A typical rally in badminton singles should consist of a serve, repeated high deep shots hit to the backline (clears) interspersed with dropshots. If and when a short clear or other type of "set-up" is forced, a smash wins the point. More often than not, an error (shuttle hit out-of-bounds or into the net) occurs rather than a positive playing finish to the rally. As a player's skill increases, he should commit fewer errors and make more outright winning plays to gain points. A player who is patient and commits few or no outright errors often wins despite the fact that he may not be spectacular. He simply waits for his opponent to err. That is badminton.

In doubles there are fewer clears, more low serves, drives, and net play. (All of these terms are described in the following text.) Again, the smash often terminates the point. As in singles, patience and the lack of unforced errors is most desirable. Team play and strategy in doubles is very important and often two players who have perfected their doubles system (rotating up and back on offense and defense) can prevail over two superior stroke players lacking in sound doubles teamwork and strategy.

SCORING

A badminton game consists of 15 points, except in ladies singles which is 11 points. The best of three games constitutes a match. Occasionally a handicap game of 21 points is played, in which case one game completes a match. The right to choose ends or to either serve or receive first in the first game of a match is decided by the toss of a coin or the spin of a racket. See page 61. If the side winning the toss chooses to serve first, the other side chooses ends, and vice versa. The sides change ends at the beginning of the second game and at the beginning of the third if a third game is necessary. In a 15-point game, ends are changed in the third game when the leading side reaches 8; in an 11-point game when either side reaches 6, ends are changed. The side that wins a game serves first in the next game.

When the game is "13 all" in singles and doubles games which consist of 15 points, the side which reached 13 first has the option of "setting" the game to 5 (a total of 18 points), and the side that scores 5 points first wins the game. The score may be set in the same manner at "14 all" for 3 points (a total of 17 points). In ladies' singles, the 11-point game may total 12 points by setting at "9 all" for 3 points or "10 all" for 2 points. Turn to chapter 7 for a more detailed description of setting. Unlike table tennis, a game does not need to be won when a player leads by 2 points. For example, the score of a match could be 15-14, 15-13, 17-16.

The game is started with an underhand stroke (serve) by a player in the right service court serving to a player in the right service court diagonally opposite. After the serve is completed, the shuttle is "in play" back and forth across the net until it touches the ground, or goes into the net, or until some other fault occurs. Points can be scored only by the serving side. Unlike tennis, the server in badminton has only one attempt to put the shuttlecock into play.

In singles, if the server fails to win the point, the score remains the same; it is then "service over," and the opposing side gains the serve and the opportunity to score. When a player has scored an even number of points, the serve must be to the right service court; when the server's score is an odd number of points, the serve is always sent to the left service court. The receiver adjusts accordingly.

In doubles, only one partner of the side that starts a game has a turn at serving in the first inning; in every subsequent inning each player on each side has a turn, the partners serving consecutively. (In baseball, an inning refers to a team's turn at bat. In badminton, both singles and doubles, an inning indicates a turn at serving for a player or players.) In doubles, when a point is scored, the server changes courts and serves to the other service court. Only the serving side changes service courts when a point is scored. The receivers remain in their same courts to allow the server to serve to the other player.

EQUIPMENT FOR BADMINTON

To play the game of badminton, you need a racket, a shuttlecock and a playing surface.

Fig. 1.1   Rackets, shuttlecocks, press and cover

Rackets   Until recently, rackets were made entirely of wood, but now those of quality are usually constructed of wood with a steel, aluminum or fiberglass shaft. Now, more players use the lighter weight metal racket strung with nylon because it can be strung more tightly with nylon than with gut. Also, metal rackets do not warp. However, there is still widespread opinion as to which is better—wood or metal.

Each brand of racket, whether made of wood, metal, aluminum or a combination of materials, offers several models to suit each player's ability to play and pay. Since the racket is the most important item of equipment, novices should ask an experienced player to help select it. The racket may be of any length or weight a player wishes.

The most popular brands are Carlton, Kawasaki, Vicort, Yonex, Sugiyama, Dunlop, Grays, Sportcraft and Kennex. Prices vary from $6 to $40 depending on whether the racket is to be used in the backyard, club, school or at the tournament level. Yonex 4500 is a good, durable metal racket for class use. For team use, Yonex 8000, Yonex 8100, Yonex 9100 and Carlton 3.7 x are recommended. Many other models are available. Some experimenting is suggested. Discounts are given for bulk purchasing.

Wood rackets are usually strung with gut and are preferred by better players because they like the 'feel.' Rackets strung with gut must be kept in a press to prevent warping. Metal rackets can be strung with gut or nylon. Nylon can be strung more tightly, lasts longer, and is less expensive. Prices range from $4 to $15 for stringing. The various brands of strings are Ashaway, Victor, Bow Brand, Yonex, Leonia, and Ballco.

When you need to replace your grip on the racket handle, there are several kinds—leather, gauze and towel, and they range in price from $1.50 to $5.25.

Shuttlecocks   The feathered shuttle used most often in tournament play is the most fragile, the most expensive and requires the most care. The most popular brands are HL Champion, Wedlo Champion, Sportcraft Tourney, Pioneer, Victor Champion, RI Tournament, Regent, and RSL. The shuttlecock must weigh from 73 to 85 grams and have fourteen to sixteen feathers attached to a kidskin-covered cork base. The feathers should be from 2 1/2 to 2 3/4 inches in length from tip to cork base and should flare at the top from 2 1/8 to 2 1/2 inches. These requirements give the shuttle its unusual, although predictable, flight patterns. Synthetic shuttles meet the foregoing specifications except that the shuttle is of nylon. A good synthetic shuttle costs slightly less than the feather shuttle and lasts many times longer.

Feathered shuttles (in tubes) should be humidified to keep them from drying and thus breaking. Nylon shuttles should be stored carefully and not left in a pile.

Carlton offers four brands of nylon shuttles: Tournament Plus, the most advanced nylon shuttle made, is available in three speeds (red for fast, blue for medium and green for slow). Tournament, for league play, is available in three speeds. Club shuttles, which come in two speeds, are the best value.

Thunderbird shuttles are made of durable nylon. A red band makes them easily visible. Three speeds are available and special speeds can be ordered. The price is $10 per dozen, but they are less expensive when purchased in quantity.

Other brands of nylon shuttles are HL True Flite, Wilson Sno Bird, Wilson Yellow Bird, Manta, EST International, Hitachi, and HL Nylon.

RSL shuttles come in two varieties: Nylon, which is excellent, is available in various speeds. Feather, generally considered the best shuttle world-wide, is used for international play. However, it is available in the United States at most reputable badminton dealers. The price is $15 per dozen with a dozen in a tube.

The Playing Surface   Measurements of the singles and doubles courts are shown in figures 1.2 and 1.3. The court is bisected by a net elevated five feet above the ground at the center and one inch higher at the posts (5'1"), which are situated on the doubles sidelines. When the game is played indoors, usually on a gymnasium floor, the ceiling of the badminton hall should not be less than twenty-six feet from the floor over the full court area. This area should be entirely free of girders and other obstructions. There should be at least four feet of clear space surrounding each court and between any two courts.

Miscellaneous Equipment   Bags to carry your racket, clothes and shuttles cost about $25. Racket covers cost about $2.50 and a racket press about the same. Badminton Fleece Balls cost $9.50 per dozen. These are made of orlon fibers and used for practice against a wall. A badminton clip board priced at $7.95 is a must for coaches to diagram plays, etc. Floor tape for marking out a court is available at $2.95 for 60 yards. A tape laying machine costs $27.95. Equipment and playing clothes are available at sporting goods stores specializing in badminton supplies. All prices, of course, are subject to change.

Badminton Equipment Specialists   For those who need equipment, the following stores offer first class supplies. These dealers fill individual or group orders by mail. They will also send catalogs and price lists. Persons at these center often know where badminton play is available in the area.

Rackets International
P.O. Box 90203
World Way Postal Center
Los Angeles, CA 90009

Louisville Badminton Supply
9411 Westport Road
Westport Plaza
Louisville, KY 40222

General Sportcraft Co., Ltd.
140 Woodbine Street
Bergenfield, NJ 07621
(201) 384-4242

Geever Sports Equipment
1010 Walnut Avenue
Des Plaines, IL 60016

Bretzke Sports
6057 E. Maple
Grand Blanc, MI 49439

World Wide Badminton Distributor
(Address same as Bretzke Sports)

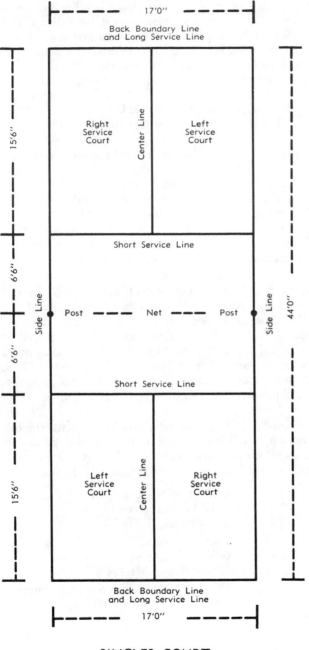

SINGLES COURT

Fig. 1.2   Singles court

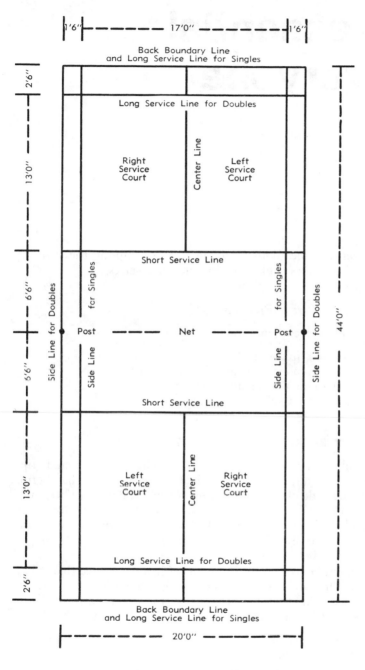

DOUBLES COURT

Fig. 1.3   Doubles court

skills essential
for everyone
2

Part I of this chapter describes skills prerequisite to attempting the stroking technique and Part II describes stroking techniques themselves.

Part I—Prerequisite Skills

Before attempting stroking technique, you must learn

> how to grip your racket
> where to position yourself on the court
> how to stand when awaiting returns
> how to move about the playing surface

HOW TO GRIP YOUR RACKET (figs. 2.1 and 2.2)

Most badminton strokes are executed with either a forehand or backhand grip. Strokes made overhead or on the right side of the body require a forehand grip. Strokes made on the left side of the body require a backhand grip. (These suggestions and instructions and others of a similar nature throughout the book pertain to right-handed players. Left-handed players should in each case use the side opposite to that cited.)

Forehand Grip   Examine your badminton racket handle. Notice that it has eight sides or bevels. The top bevel is the side of the handle which is visible when the racket head is held at right angles to the ground, as shown in figure 2.1. Here are nine points to remember in holding the racket for this grip:

1. The point of the V formed by your thumb and forefinger is on the top bevel of the eight-sided handle.
2. Hold the racket in your fingers. Do not palm it.
3. Lay the handle diagonally across your fingers and palm and let your little finger maintain a firm hold.

Fig. 2.1   Forehand grip

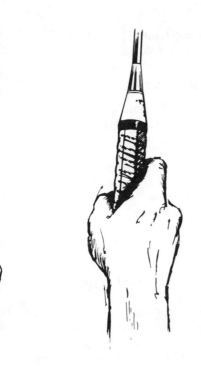

Fig. 2.2   Backhand grip

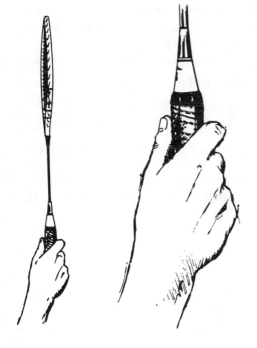

4. Hold the racket as near the end of the handle as possible. This allows you to achieve more wrist action.
5. Do not let the butt of the handle extend outside the heel of your hand.
6. Spread your fingers so they are comfortable, particularly the forefinger and third finger.
7. Use your thumb and forefinger to control the racket.
8. When you execute power shots, hold the racket firmly at impact.
9. On "touch" shots, hold the racket more loosely.

To get a comfortable feeling it may be necessary to adjust this basic grip by spreading or closing your fingers, by moving your hand closer to the end, or by resting the end of the handle at a comfortable place on the heel of your hand.

Remember: The position of the V should not be changed.

Backhand Grip   For this grip (for shots played on the left side of the body), remember these three points:

1. Turn your hand counterclockwise until the point of the V is on the top left bevel.
2. Most important, place the ball of your thumb flat against the back bevel of the handle. This thumb position gives the support needed to gain speed on drives and depth on clears.
3. Since dropshots and net shots demand control rather than power, it is not necessary to have your thumb flat. In fact, the side of your thumb may rest along the back bevel as it does on the forehand.

How is the backhand grip for a net shot changed to perform a backhand high clear? Why is this change in hand position advocated?

WHERE TO POSITION YOURSELF ON THE COURT

The center location is your basic position. This is the location on the court from which you are able to reach most shots easily. Here, you command the best area for any maneuver.

The center location is halfway from the net and back boundary line and halfway from the sidelines.

Your opponent will try to draw you from this basic center position by directing the shuttle to a corner. Your strategy is to retrieve the corner shots but return quickly to the center position.

HOW TO STAND WHEN AWAITING RETURNS

To ready yourself for each of your opponents strokes, remember these nine points:

1. Take a position in the center of the court. Stand alertly with your weight evenly distributed on the balls of your feet.

2. Your feet should be apart just enough to give good balance, but not so far apart that movement is restricted.
3. Knees should be slightly flexed and easy, ready for instantaneous action.
4. Relax your body. Don't hold it stiff and upright.
5. Carry both your arms in front of your body with the racket acting almost as a shield to keep the shuttle from getting past.
6. Hold the racket head up about shoulder height in front of and away from your body in order to allow a swift strike.
7. Experiment to determine the best position for you.
8. Concentrate on the shuttle as it is leaving your opponent's racket and try to determine the direction of the attack or defense.
9. As soon as you determine the direction, move your feet and pivot your body by the time the shuttle crosses the net.

All players vary the ready position somewhat to suit their own style and comfort. Champions adjust it to give them the greatest mobility and quickness. Quickness refers not only to feet and hands but to eyes and brains as well. The shuttle has such a short distance to travel that it will come swiftly and offer you little time to execute the fundamentals.

In fact, in badminton, absolutely no time is available to pause and survey the situation. Even in doubles, where your partner covers half the court, you must be ready for every shot. Points are made because opponents have neither the time nor the reflexes to get their rackets in position to return the shuttle.

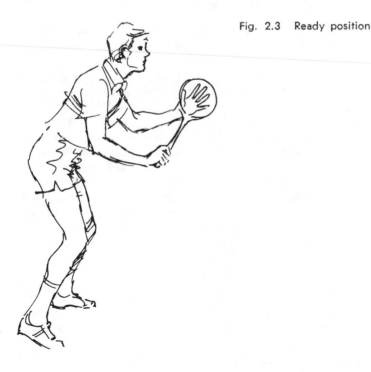

Fig. 2.3   Ready position

HOW TO MOVE ABOUT THE PLAYING SURFACE

In order to get within reach of the shuttlecock, good footwork is essential. Powerful and deceptive strokes are of little use if a player is not in the correct place soon enough to stroke the shuttle effectively.

Essentials of Moving About the Playing Surface

1. The beginning of good footwork is an alert starting position. Keep the body ready to move in any direction by flexing the knees slightly with your weight on the forward part of your feet. Think "ready." A stiff upright stance does not indicate or permit speed. "Bouncing" best describes badminton footwork.
2. To move to the baseline, take a sideways skipping action with your feet kept close to the floor.
3. To hit a forehand or overhead stroke in the deep right court, skip diagonally back to your right. Lead with your right foot. Finish with your left side partially turned toward the net. Your left foot is forward as you hit.
4. To play a backhand drive or clear from the deep left court, skip diagonally back, left foot leading. Your right side is toward the net. Your right foot is diagonally forward.
5. It is very important not to be moving when your opponent hits the shuttle.
6. If you cannot get completely back to the center of the court, pause where you are before your opponent hits the shuttle.

When moving from center to various parts of the court, step with the right foot first when moving to the right—whether forward, backward, or to the side. Step with the left foot first when moving to any part of the left side.

Right foot is the racket foot in badminton. Unlike tennis, most shots are played "off" the right foot (that is, the right leg and foot have the weight on them at the moment of contact) even when playing shots on the right side of the court. This allows for better reach, without getting too far from the center of the court. After playing the shot, push off the right toward center position.

As your footwork skills become more proficient, the number of steps from center to all parts of the court can be determined. The footwork then becomes a pattern. Learning to judge whether or not a shuttle is going out of bounds on the baseline and sidelines is made easier when the footwork becomes measured. The easiest part of badminton footwork is, of course, running forward. Because the basic waiting position is in the center of the court, however, backward and sideward steps are also required. Moving backward is called "backpedaling." It is a skill demanded in other sports, too. The "T" formation quarterback backpedals almost every time he takes the ball from the center.

Which is more important, to be standing still when your opponent strikes the shuttlecock or to get back to the center of your court area before the opponent's shot crosses the net?

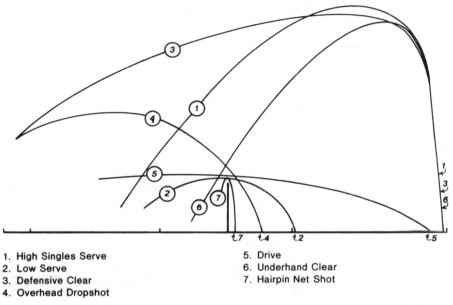

1. High Singles Serve
2. Low Serve
3. Defensive Clear
4. Overhead Dropshot
5. Drive
6. Underhand Clear
7. Hairpin Net Shot

Fig. 2.4   Flight patterns

So it is with the badminton player. Keep your head and eyes forward at all times. If you have to return and run with your back to the net, you will not have enough time to turn again to stroke the shuttle.

Good footwork combined with early anticipation of the direction and depth of the shuttlecock should place the player *behind* the shuttle. This enables a move forward and a hit into the shot. Sluggish footwork often results in the shuttle getting behind the player, resulting in a poorly executed stroke. Good footwork is not only important in returning high deep clears but essential for an effective return of a high deep serve.

Part II—Stroking Techniques

Mastering the fundamental stroking techniques involves, specifically:

> how to serve
> how to get a good overhead clear
> how to produce a good dropshot
> how to play a good drive
> how to hit the underhand stroke
> how to play at the net

HOW TO SERVE

Begin play with the serve, an underhand stroke. Play it underhand forehand or underhand backhand, although underhand forehand is the usual method. The shaft of the racket must now point downward so that the whole of the head of the racket is discernibly below the hand holding the racket. (See figure 2.5, below.)

Practice moving from center court to the right and left sidelines and to the baseline until you are consistent in the number of steps taken for a given direction. How many steps do you require to play the shuttle from each of the three boundary lines?

Basic Singles Serve

1. Take a comfortable position in the court about three feet behind the short service line and to the right or left of the centerline.
2. Stand with your feet spread but not so far apart that you cannot move quickly.
3. Your left foot should be in advance of your right foot.
4. Both feet must remain in contact with the floor until you contact the shuttle.
5. Once you put your racket in motion to serve, neither foot may slide during the entire execution of the stroke.
6. Hold the shuttle at the base between your thumb and forefinger of your left hand (or use both fore and middle fingers). Extend your arm forward about level with your shoulders.
7. Hold the racket with a forehand grip with your wrist cocked. Bring the racket behind your body at about waist level. This is the starting position. Then drop the shuttle.

Fig. 2.5   Serve

Fig. 2.6   Mistakes most commonly made with the serve

8. Swing the racket forward to the contact point at about knee level. Uncock the wrist and let the racket and shuttle meet ahead of your body between knee and waist level.
9. Rapidly rotate the forearm and wrist inward immediately after contact. Most strokes in badminton are made with a similar rotating movement.
10. The follow-through goes in the direction that you intend the shuttle to go, that is, high and deep. Avoid bringing the racket up to the shuttle. Let the shuttle drop. Otherwise an outright miss or a wood shot (hitting the frame of the racket) result.

The Low Serve   The low serve is used almost exclusively in doubles and with great variation. The grips and stance are usually the same as for the singles serve, but the racket pattern and use of the wrist are almost indescribable. Of all the strokes in badminton, the low serve technique has the most variables. The swing is often shortened and the stroke made almost entirely with your wrist guiding the shuttle. Other players prefer an exceptionally firm wrist believing it gives more control. This is one stroke a player must experiment with and find the style best suited for him. Try for accuracy in having the shuttle go over the top of the net with minimum clearance. If your low serve forces the receiver to hit up it is a highly successful serve. If the receiver "rushes" your low serve and is able to hit it on the downswing, change your technique and practice it more.

Placement Areas (fig. 2.7)   As shown in figure 2.5, the serve can be directed high or low, short or long. Figure 2.7 shows the specific areas within the service court to which the shuttle can be served most effectively.

    In singles there should be no noticeable difference in the way one produces low and high serves, as here again deception is important in order to keep your opponent in doubt as to which it will be (and off balance). Basically, the high

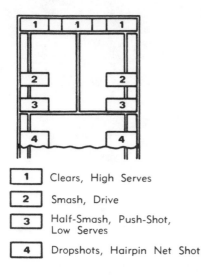

Fig. 2.7   Placement areas

1	Clears, High Serves
2	Smash, Drive
3	Half-Smash, Push-Shot, Low Serves
4	Dropshots, Hairpin Net Shot

serve is used more often in singles and the low serve more often in doubles. Occasionally mixing them keeps your opponent uncertain and unable to predict your pattern. It is imperative that you serve well, as serving gives you the opportunity to score.

Even though somewhat alike in production, the low and high serves are different. They can be compared with the dropshot and clear in wrist action and needed power. The low serve takes little power and is almost guided over the net whereas the high, deep serve will take all the strength and power available to get the shuttle high enough and deep enough to be considered successful. It has much the same flight as the clear because it is hit to a point high above the backcourt and when it loses speed it turns and falls straight down. If the shuttle falls straight down on the back boundary line, the opponent must be that far back in the court to return it. If it is too flat and too low, the receiver will intercept it before it ever gets to the backcourt.

Conversely, the shuttle hit with a low serve has a flat arc as it just skims over the net and into the court near the short service line.

The low serve in doubles requires the same grip and foot position. However, the backswing is shortened, the shuttle contacted as near waist level as possible and perhaps slightly more to the right. The shuttle is guided over the net without wrist motion. A great deal less shoulder, arm and wrist power will be needed to hit the short distance and low trajectory required for the low serve.

Because the serve is played underhand and therefore must be hit upward, it is considered a defensive stroke. Consequently, in order to score, the server must eventually turn his defense into an attack. Since the receiver cannot score a point, his objective is to stay on the attack and win the opportunity to serve, making it possible then for him to score. This peculiarity of badminton—having to score from a beginning defensive position—prolongs a game even though no points are recorded.

HOW TO GET A GOOD OVERHEAD CLEAR

The clear is a high shot to the back of the court. It may be offensive or defensive. Generally, offensive shots arc hit down. The attacking clear is the exception to this rule.

Fig. 2.8   Overhead clear

Fig. 2.9   Mistakes most commonly made with the overhead clear

Procedure

1. Take the proper forehand grip, watch the approaching shuttle, and use the prescribed footwork. Move yourself to a place where you are in correct relationship to the shuttle.
2. As you are moving to this position behind the shuttle, swing your racket and arm back behind your head and shoulders. This will require pivoting at your waist and turning your shoulders sideways to the net. This position is fundamentally the same as that taken by a baseball outfielder making an overarm throw to home plate. In badminton the racket, instead of the ball, is your hand, but it is literally thrown at the shuttle in the identical fashion.
3. Rotate your forearm and wrist inward as you move the racket from behind your head. This rotation continues through the entire stroke.
4. Incorrectly allowing your arm to drop and bend when stroking results in loss of power. With full power, contact the shuttle with your arm fully extended and ahead of your body.
5. Rotate your trunk forward during this stroke to gain power.
6. Your ideal position is behind and in line with the shuttle.
7. Always hit the shuttle as soon as possible so that your opponent will not have time to get your shots.
8. Meet the shuttle with a flat racket or surface without any cutting or slicing motion. Cutting gives control but takes away power.

Here are some additional suggestions for achieving a successful clear.

1. Since the shuttlecock is difficult to slice because of its feathers and does not react as a spinning ball, it is essential to learn how to exert power.
2. The contact of the racket and shuttle must be quite explosive to get distance since there is little weight on the racket.
3. The angle of the racket face upon contact is the final determining factor as to the direction the shuttle will take.
4. Be sure to move your weight into the shot as the stroke is made.
5. Note the flight pattern of the clear in figure 2.4. The shuttle is hit high enough so that a certain point, almost above the back boundary line, it loses speed and turns and falls straight down. A shuttle falling at right angles to the floor is most difficult to play. It is important to hit the shuttle with depth because your opponent will be unable to smash a clear effectively from the back boundary line.

High Clear Strategy   The high deep or defensive clear is used primarily to gain time for the player to return to the center position in the court. One of the most valuable benefits of this shot is derived from its use in combinations with the dropshot to run your opponent, making him defend all four corners of the court.

As can be seen in figure 2.4, depth and height of the shuttlecock are extremely important on the defensive clear in order to force your opponent as far into the backcourt as possible.

Your next shot, a dropshot just over the net, would become very effective in this game of maneuvering for openings and spaces. It might also force your opponent to hit a short return which could be smashed. It takes a strong player to clear from one baseline to the opposite one and an extraordinarily strong player to high clear cross court to the diagonal corner. Unless a shuttle that flies very fast is used, it is unlikely that the average player would be able to accomplish this difficult feat. Consequently, in singles, the player who hits a high deep defensive clear gains control of the rally and should eventually win that point.

In analyzing a match played by contestants of equal skill, the player who consistently has good length always wins. When playing, if you find you do not have time to reach the shots and each point is a struggle, then check the length of your clears. Your opponent will seldom return a winning shot or putaway if your clear is deep enough. Also, clears that are too low and too short are cut off before they reach the backcourt.

The Attacking Clear   After learning the basic high deep clear, the attacking clear, a modification, can be developed. Its use should not be confused with that of the defensive clear or disaster will result.

1. The trajectory of the attacking clear is not as high but it is faster. There is a different arc to the flight pattern, as can be seen in figure 3.1.
2. Because the arc is low, the opponent must be drawn out of the center position before the attacking clear can be used successfully.
3. Often the attacking clear is best used following a good dropshot to the forehand corner. The clear can then be hit quickly to the backhand corner while the opponent is recovering from the net.
4. Once the clear gets behind the opponent on the backhand, the return is almost sure to be in the forecourt. When an opponent's return is forced to be short, the point should be yours!
5. A defensive clear incorrectly used in this situation would give the opponent time to move back and hit overhead and your advantage would be lost.

The only difference in the production of these two types of clears is that the attacking clear has a flatter arc; therefore, stroke it with less upward angle. It also requires less power, since without the height there is less distance to travel.

Care must be taken when standing near the net that the flat clear is not sent out over the back boundary line. It necessitates controlled power and yet it has to be fast enough to get behind the opponent.

HOW TO PRODUCE A GOOD DROPSHOT

The dropshot is a slow shot that drops just over the net in the opponent's forecourt.

Procedure

1. Use exactly the same grip, footwork, body position, and backswing described for the overhead clear. Indeed, your intention should be to suggest that a clear is forthcoming.

2. The difference is wrist speed. There is still full wrist rotation but the shuttle is stroked with greater control rather than "patted."
3. Contact the shuttle farther ahead of your body in order to direct it downward.
4. The downward movement of your arm coupled with completion of your wrist action brings the shuttle down.
5. Tilt the face of the racket downward at the angle you wish the shuttle to take.
6. Rotate your shoulder and trunk forward and move your weight into the shot.

Which stroke and which flight path require the greatest power in badminton?

Advantages of a Dropshot

1. A dropshot is invaluable because it enables you to use the front corners of the court. No other type of shot goes to the two front corners near the net.
2. The smash and drive are placed midcourt or deeper as shown in figures 2.4 and 3.1. Always place the dropshot in the forecourt. The dropshot, whether overhead, underhand or hit from the side can be played from any place on the court.

Dropshot Strategy

1. A major part of singles strategy lies in using the overhead dropshot in combination with clears. For example, if clears are used repeatedly, a player tends

Fig. 2.10   Overhead dropshot

Fig. 2.11   Mistakes most commonly made with the overhead dropshot

    to move his basic position toward the rear of the court in order to cover the deep shots. This position makes the dropshot doubly effective.

2. Singles becomes a game of up and back and up and back again until a weak return is forced and a smash finishes the rally.

3. A midcourt shot, one which is halfway between the net and back boundary line, obviously is not as useful in singles as in doubles, since these shots do not move the opponent out of center. Consequently, keep the shuttle as far from the center of the court as possible with clears and drops.

4. Deception is the most outstanding characteristic of a good dropshot. If the dropshot is deceptive enough it can be an outright winner even though it might have been planned as a lead-up shot.

5. If your opponent is halfway to the net or at the net before your shot reaches the net, then you haven't fooled him and you have probably lost the exchange.

6. As you become more skilled with the dropshot, experiment by hitting it fast or slow and with more or less arc. Try slicing the shuttle slightly in order to slow it down and change its direction. This will very much add to the deception of the shot.

7. The least attractive characteristic of the dropshot is its slow flight. Anything moving slowly unfortunately gives your opponent what you don't want him to have—time. The dropshot, however, contributes to the essence of the game—measuring time and selecting shots in relation to your own and your opponent's position on the court.

Angle of the Racket Face   The direction of the shuttle's flight in all overhead shots is determined by the angle of the racket face. Bringing the wrist and racket head through too soon causes an extreme downward angle to the shuttle, often resulting in a netted shot. Conversely, failure to bring the wrist and racket head through soon enough causes an extreme upward angle. See the illustration below.

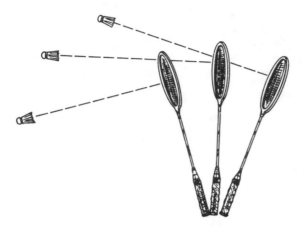

Fig. 2.12   Angle of racket face

Can you name the two most important characteristics of a good dropshot?

HOW TO PLAY A GOOD DRIVE

The drive is a flat sidearm stroke played as a forehand or backhand.

Forehand Drive   The forehand drive is played on the right side of the body and is similar to the baseball sidearm throw.

1. Take a forehand grip, turn your body until your left shoulder is to the net, place the left foot forward, and turn your shoulders to allow your arm to take the backswing.
2. Place the head of the racket between your shoulder blades. To start the backswing, bend your elbow and cock your wrist backward in preparation for a big, powerful swing.
3. Watch the shuttle closely with the idea of contacting it diagonally ahead between shoulder and waist height.
4. As your arm and racket swing forward, your body weight should transfer from your right foot to your left foot. Rotate your forearm and wrist inward during the stroke.
5. Contact the shuttle with a flat racket face and well away from you so that your swing is not restricted.
6. Swing the racket on through in the direction of the flight of the shuttle. The speed of your swing compels the racket to complete its follow-through past the left shoulder. The racket has practically made a 360° circle. The action of the swing, particularly in the contact area, is explosive.

Fig. 2.13   Forehand drive

Fig. 2.14   Mistakes most commonly made with the forehand
drive

7. On many occasions, the forehand drive is played with the *right* foot extended toward the sideline. This allows for a further reach without getting too far from the center position.

Backhand Drive   The backhand drive employs the same basic principles as the forehand drive with two or three exceptions:

1. The grip is changed to the backhand grip, making sure that your thumb is flat on the handle. Now, rotate your forearm and wrist outward.
2. Elbow action is important in this and all other strokes. On the backswing your elbow is bent, your right hand is at your left shoulder, and your elbow is pointing at the oncoming shuttle.
3. Your weight shifts, your shoulders turn, your arm starts swinging forward with your elbow leading, and then the head of the racket whips through for the contact and follow-through.

Fig. 2.15   Backhand drive

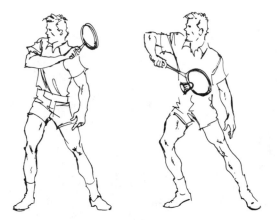

Fig. 2.16   Mistakes most commonly made with the backhand
drive

Playing the Drives   Long, deep, fast drives and slower paced midcourt drives
can be played from either side of the body. Drives can be played like other shots,
from one sideline diagonally across the court to the other sideline (crosscourt)
or they can be played parallel to the sideline (down-the-line). The flight pattern
of the drive is parallel to the floor and the shuttle just skims the net. See figure
2.4. The drive is played anywhere from midcourt to backcourt and is driven to
your opponent's midcourt depending on his location in the court at the
moment.

The higher you can contact the shuttle on the drive, the less you will have
to hit up. For example, if you hit the shuttle from below knee level it will have
to go up to get over the net and will continue to rise as it carries on to midcourt.

If the shuttle rises to net level and then turns toward the floor because
speed is lost, you have mistakenly hit a dropshot. Any shot higher than net level

can be smashed and therein lies the danger of the hard hit drive played from a low contact point. A drive less powerful (midcourt) may be of value if your opponent is not pulled out of position. The shuttle's arc will reach its peak at the net and descend from there on to midcourt. It therefore cannot be smashed.

Try never to provide your opponent with a set-up for a smash.

Use the fast drive when an opponent is out of position and you wish to get the shuttle behind him to the backcourt. Perhaps you hit a well-placed dropshot to his forehand. The deep backhand corner is now briefly open. If your opponent returns your dropshot to your forehand, your problem is simple. If he plays it down-the-line to your backhand, it is not so simple. You must get the shuttle there quickly before he gains the center of the court or he will block the shot off for a winner while you are still recovering from the execution of your stroke. It takes more time to recover body balance and center position from hard hit power shots than from dropshots, midcourt drives, or net shots.

If the two kinds of drive are used correctly and intelligently, they can be valuable attacking weapons. Used badly, they can cause disaster.

Angle of the Racket Face   The direction of the shuttle's flight is determined by the angle of the racket face. It will require a great deal of practice to learn to control the moment of impact of the racket head and the shuttle in order to direct shots down-the-line or crosscourt.

HOW TO HIT THE UNDERHAND STROKES

Underhand strokes are, like the serve, those in which the contact point and the entire head of the racket are below the level of the hand. The contact point is below net level which necessitates an upward stroke.

Underhand Clear   Many of the same stroke production fundamentals of the high, deep, singles serve—the grip, the footwork, the wrist and arm power, and the follow-through—can be applied to the underhand clear. When stroking this clear, swing the racket down from the ready position, under the shuttle for contact and up, following through in the intended direction of the shuttle. Except for the fact that it originates near the net, the flight pattern the shuttle makes mimics the high, deep serve. Note figure 2.4.

Just as with the overhead defensive clear, use the underhand clear to gain time to recover the center position and to force the opponent to the backcourt. The underhand clear's values are many in both singles and doubles. For example, if a dropshot is not particularly good and does not fall close to the net, a large choice of shots is available. Near-perfect dropshots necessitate a return with an underhand clear, in which case this stroke becomes indispensable. The only alternative to using the underhand clear is the hairpin net shot described on page 28.

Underhand Dropshot   The underhand dropshot described here is played from an area between the short service line and the baseline to the opponent's side of the net as near to the net as possible. It has specific use both in singles and doubles.

Closely related, and yet different in its usage, is the dropshot played closer to the net. See figure 2.4. The fundamentals of stroking and the characteristics of the underhand dropshot are almost identical with those of the low serve. A slow, controlled shot, the dropshot has its limitations for this reason: if you hit the shuttle from the baseline at a slow pace, your opponent has time to pounce on it at the net. Unless the underhand dropshot is disguised, ineffective returns result. Although rarely played successfully from the baseline, this stroke's values are exceptional in doubles and mixed doubles when played from midcourt. In doubles, the dropshot is used to run the net player from side to side or to draw a player up when both players are back. In singles, it can be a superb return of a smash. Directed crosscourt away from the smasher, the dropshot forces him to recover quickly and to run the long distance.

With all strokes, the learning process is the slow, gradual one of getting increased accuracy, further depth, and additional speed. As you continue to play and practice, the shuttle will travel increasingly more often in the direction in which you aim it. You will attain more and more power in clears and smashes and (desirably) less and less speed in dropshots. To further help you stroke your shots effectively and with care, correctly executed basic positions and footwork must precede the actual stroke production. The entire process, then, is one of smooth coordination.

In every sport involving eye-hand contact, there is one fundamental principle which cannot be overemphasized. In the case of golf or tennis it is "keep your eye on the ball." In badminton it is "keep your eye on the shuttlecock." If you do not watch the shuttlecock, one of the following mistakes will occur:

1. You will miss the shuttlecock entirely.
2. You will hit the feathers of the shuttlecock.
3. You will not hit the shuttle in the center of the racket, thus causing a throw, sling, or a carry.

HOW TO PLAY AT THE NET

Description   Net play is a general term encompassing those shots played from the area around the short service line to the net. See figure 2.17. Net play, which includes the hairpin net shot described in this chapter as well as the push shot and the smash described in chapter 3, is very important because the front of the court has to be defended.

The forehand grip is generally satisfactory for net play but the backhand grip must be adjusted slightly:

1. The side of the thumb is placed up the back bevel of the racket which may cause a slight turning of the hand toward the forehand grip.
2. The wrist is used differently for net shots, that is, with little relationship to the shoulders and body. The grip adjustment allows such wrist action. Conversely, this grip could not be used successfully to perform a clear from the backhand corner.

On both forehand and backhand strokes, spread the fingers and hold the racket almost loosely. This should give more "touch." To get even more control, hold the racket slightly up from the end. This shortening of the grip gives less power (not needed at net) and less reach. You must decide, therefore, what you wish to gain (control) and what you wish to sacrifice (reach).

The feet, body, and upper arm are used for reaching rather than for stroke production; the actual strokes are done with the forearm, wrist, and hand. The racket meets the shuttle with a flat face. The wrist action may be smooth and controlled or it may be quick, depending on the type of net shot you are attempting. The explosive power so essential for clears and smashes is not needed in the forecourt.

The follow-through should be in the direction in which you wish the shuttle to travel. Guide it and go with it. At times, the follow-through must be abbreviated to avoid hitting the net. According to the rules, a player may not hit the net as long as the shuttle is in play. It is in play until it hits the net or floor.

Your court position for net play in singles and doubles should be such that your extended arm and racket can just touch the net. This distance from the net will permit unrestricted movement of your arm. In doubles it will also enable you to cover more midcourt shots.

What is the role of the feet, body, and upper arm when executing a net shot?

In net play take fast, small steps which allow you to turn and move quickly in any direction. The left foot should be forward on forehand shots and the right foot on the backhand ones. In exceptional cases, the right foot may be forward when that extra bit of reach is needed to get to the shuttle on the forehand side.

The most difficult shots to play at net are those which are falling perpendicular to the floor rather than diagonally. Diagonally dropping shuttles arrive farther back in the court; perpendicular falling shuttles, at their best, touch or

Fig. 2.17   Net play

almost touch the net as they fall toward the floor. These are extremely difficult to play, and since they cannot be directed forward, only upward, they are called hairpin net shots. Your opponent, sensing this, is alert to smash as soon as the shuttle comes up and over the net.

Hairpin Net Shot   The hairpin net shot gets its name from the flight pattern of the shuttle. See figure 2.4. Played from one side of the net to the other, it should fall perpendicular to the floor and close to the net on the opponent's side. This shot travels the least distance of any badminton shot; consequently, very little stroke is needed. The shuttle played at net level may be tapped or blocked back. Played well below net level, it will have to be stroked with great care up and over the net. Some championship players stroke the shuttle with a slicing action which gives the shuttle less speed and a spinning motion that is difficult to return. The perfect hairpin shot results in the shuttle's crawling up and over the net and trickling down the other side.

better players
master these
techniques
3

It is fun to experiment with additional strokes to use in combination with the essential skills described in chapter 2. Descriptions of advanced strokes such as the half-smash, backhand smash, the round-the-head shot, the driven serve, the push shot, net smash, and the backhand serve will be found in this chapter. Many of these strokes are no more difficult to execute than the basic ones, but they are variations and are easier once the basic strokes are mastered. Dwelling too soon on spectacular shots at the expense of the standard, traditional ones that are used most of the time, tends to be frustrating and discouraging once the player is in a true contest of skills as any good badminton game offers.

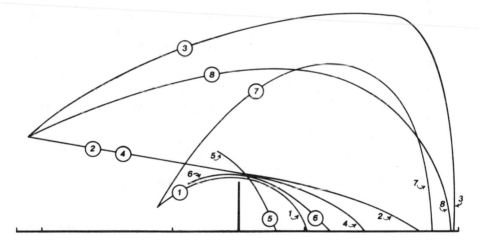

1. Backhand Serve
2. Smash
3. Backhand Clear
4. Half Smash

5. Net Smash
6. Push Shot
7. High Doubles Serve
8. Attacking Clear

Fig. 3.1   Flight patterns

Nevertheless, as you gain experience and perfect your basic strokes, you will want to add threat to your game. The fact that your opponent must be alert to this possibility further assures the effectiveness of the basic strokes. In this chapter, you will learn the following:

how to smash
how to backhand clear
how to make a round-the-head shot
how to play a driven serve
how to backhand serve
how to "hold the shuttle"
how to play more difficult net shots

HOW TO SMASH

The smash is a powerful overhead shot used to "put away" any shuttle above the height of the net.

1. In the interest of deception, the smash should be masked as a clear or a drop. Use the same grip, footwork, body position, backswing, and contact point as with the clear and the drop, and your opponent will not anticipate your return.
2. The smash differs from the clear and the dropshot in that it can be hit only from an overhead position; a clear and a dropshot can be either an overhead or underhanded shot.
3. Be sure you move yourself to a position behind the shuttle as quickly as possible.
4. Take care to have a proper body position, since balance must be perfect to achieve maximum power from your shoulders, arms, and wrist.
5. Your left shoulder must be turned to the net and your right shoulder back and ready to strike with force.
6. Cock your arm and wrist behind your body ready to unleash all available power. The racket head may be moving at a terrific rate as it goes out to meet the shuttle. The handle must be gripped quite firmly at the instant of contact.
7. Contact the shuttle at the highest possible point. The follow-through is down and in line with the flight of the shuttle.
8. Hit the overhead smash with as much power as that needed for the high, deep clear. To get such power, rotate the wrist and forearm fully and rapidly and use perfect timing.
9. Rotate your trunk and shoulders forward and throw your weight into the shot. When you are first learning to smash, however, try to get your timing and downward angle correct before attempting to get excessive speed. Timing is thrown off if too much arm and body effort are involved in the stroke.
10. The racket face must be angled downward at contact point to make the shuttle travel sharply downward.
11. It is important to remember that the farther away you are from the net, the less angle and speed the smash can carry.

Fig. 3.2   Smash

Fig. 3.3   Mistakes most commonly made with the smash

Strategy   Two reasons for using a smash are:

1. It has more downward angle and speed than any other stroke, making it
    the main point-winning shot. If the pattern of play has developed as
    planned, your final stroke of the rally will be in an overhead smash.

2. If the smash is returned, the return will be (because of the angle of your smash) an upward (defensive) stroke.

Obviously, in both situations, the smash is an invaluable weapon. There is, however, a reason for avoiding indiscriminate use of the smash; namely, the effort needed to smash leaves your body off balance, and therefore it takes longer to recover your position than with other types of shots. Thus, your judgment as to when to smash rather than to clear or to drop is important. Many factors related to you and to your opponent will enter into this decision.

It is interesting to note the characteristics which are alike in making the various shots. See figures 2.8 and 2.10. The position of the feet and the body is the same for all overhead shots. The stroke pattern—backswing, forward swing, and follow-through—should also be almost identical for the overhead strokes in order to employ the deception necessary to make the shots effective. What, then, determines whether an overhead shot is to be a clear, a dropshot, or a smash?

The answer lies in the speed of the wrist, the degree of wrist action used, and the angle of the face of the racket at the moment of contact with the shuttle. On all badminton shots, cock the wrist back ready for the action that comes within the larger action of the shoulder and arm swing. Wrist power alone is not sufficient to propel the shuttle from one end of the court to the other; it necessitates arm power and shoulder rotation in addition to exact timing of the wrist snap as the weight moves forward. When a player intends to smash and put the shuttle "away," he may leap off the ground for better angle and possible added power. In this case, he is not using any deception to enhance the stroke. Total energy is being called upon instead.

The Half-Paced Smash   The half-paced smash, popularly called "half-smash," is simply a smash with less speed. The elements of stroke production related to the smash, described in chapter 2 and figures 3.1 and 3.2, apply to the half-smash. It is important to keep the following points in mind:

1. The half-smash is played by contacting the shuttle with an extended arm diagonally above the head in order to obtain a steep angle downward.
2. To cut or slice the half-smash diminishes its speed and makes the shuttle fall close to the net at a sharper angle.
3. If the shuttle gets behind the player, the racket will be facing upward at contact point, the flight of the shuttle will be upward, and the shot will be a defensive one, in all probability a clear. It is important, therefore, that the shuttle be contacted well ahead of the body.
4. Caution: A smash hit with a bent arm results in loss of power and angle. The smash is then known as a "flat" smash, a highly undesirable shot.

The half-smash has as many values as the full, powerful smash, but is of a different nature. The half-smash can be played with less effort. Moreover, it can be played from deeper in the court since recovery of balance does not present a problem. Moving to cover the net return after the half-smash can be accomplished with ease. By contrast, a full smash from the backcourt leaves the front corners vulnerable. The use of the half-smash therefore is less risky. It is valuable, too, because of its sharply angled downward direction. By hitting downward, the attack is gained by forcing the opponent to stroke upward. Very few points are won outright from an underhand stroke. The ones that are can be attributed to outright deception or to outpositioning the opponent.

HOW TO BACKHAND CLEAR

The backhand clear is a high, deep shot played from the left side of the court.

Procedure

1. Use the backhand grip with the ball of the thumb flat against the back bevel as described for the backhand drive.
2. The feet and body positions are identical with the drive.
3. At the completion of the backswing, the elbow should be pointing at the oncoming shuttle.
4. The most important aspect of the swing is the timing of the wrist as it swings the head of the racket forward to meet the shuttle (at just the right instant).
5. Be sure to rotate the trunk and shoulders into the shot.

Fig. 3.4   Backhand clear

Fig. 3.5   Mistakes most commonly made with the backhand clear

Strategy   For many players, the backhand clear from deep court is the most difficult of all shots. Excellent timing and power are essential to clear the shuttle high enough and deep enough to make it a safe shot. The high deep shot to the left side of the court could be played with a round-the-head shot or overhead clear, but the player's court position would be sacrificed. A player must assess his own capabilities before selecting the particular stroke to use.

HOW TO PRODUCE A ROUND-THE-HEAD SHOT

Description

The round-the-head shot is another overhead shot and an unusual one because it is played on the left or backhand side of the body. It may be a clear, a half-smash, or a dropshot. The execution of the round-the-head stroke is closely related to that of overhead strokes. See chapter 2 for instructions.

Procedure

1. One major difference from the overhead stroke is that the contact point is above your left shoulder, necessitating a reach to the left and a bend of the knees and body.
2. The shot is played with your body facing the net and the weight on the left foot and the palm of the hand facing the net when the racket contacts the shuttle.
3. The right leg and weight swing forward for the follow-through of the stroke.

   The description and execution of the round-the-head stroke make it seem more difficult than it actually is.

Strategy   Many sound reasons can be found for taking the shuttlecock with a round-the-head stroke rather than with a backhand stroke. First, more power is possible overhead than on the backhand, which, in turn, results in better depth and speed on the shuttle. In addition, since the opponent will be attack-

Fig. 3.6   Round-the-head shot

Fig. 3.7   Mistakes most commonly made with the round-the-head shot

ing the backhand corner, it is imperative that the area be protected at every opportunity. The round-the-head shot meets this need. For example, if a low clear or driven serve to the backhand side can be anticipated, it can be intercepted with a round-the-head shot.

Not all the results of this shot are favorable, however, as the feet and body will have to be moved to the left side of the court to guard the backhand area, and a large portion of the forehand side of the court will be left open. Advantages gained by this maneuver will have to be weighed against the disadvantages. The strength of your backhand and your speed of foot will be determining factors in selecting the round-the-head instead of the backhand. The ideal player will be able to play the high backhand shot as well as the round-the-head shot.

HOW TO PLAY THE DRIVEN SERVE

Elements of the Driven Serve

1. The weak return is the desired outcome of a good driven serve.
2. Sheer speed and force of shot will not be enough for success.
3. Very few points are won outright on the driven serve, or on any serve, since it is played from an underhand (defensive) position.
4. If the driven serve can jolt your opponent off balance and thus place you in an offensive position, the immediate objective has been achieved.
5. The mistake made by an ambitious receiver upon returning a good driven serve is to try to do too much with it. If the shuttle has carried behind the receiver as the server has planned it, the receiver should be content to play a safe, high, deep clear in order to regain balance. This serve will not be so effective if your opponent's speed of reflexes is exceptionally good.
6. Against a player of different capabilities or against a player whose court position is faulty, the driven serve may be the answer to a serving problem.

What are the advantages of the half-smash over the smash and the backhand stroke over the round-the-head stroke?

Strategy   The driven serve, most frequently used in doubles, has a specific value to a side-by-side (defensive) team. The angle that can be attained by serving from a position near the sideline can make an aggressive return almost impossible.

In conclusion, the effectiveness of the driven serve is due to its angle, speed, and some degree of deception. It must be noted here that the deception must be in the wrist. Any preliminary movements of the body intended to fool the receiver are illegal on the serve. If the server delays hitting the shuttle for so long as to be unfair to the receiver, it is a fault. This faulty tactic, called a balk, is further described in the rules in chapter 7, page 64.

HOW TO BACKHAND SERVE

This serve is a common stroke to Asian players and is now gaining popularity elsewhere.

Procedure

1. Use a backhand grip—shortened to give more control.
2. Place right foot forward.
3. Hold shuttle in front of the body with the base pointed toward the racket.
4. Stroke the shuttle gently over the net towards the short serviceline.

Fig. 3.8   Backhand serve

Strategy   The backhand serve is a useful service variation because:

1. It can be changed easily to a flick service to the back of the court.
2. It is hit in front of the body and takes very little time to reach its destination.
3. The shuttle is hard to see against the server's white clothes.

HOW TO "HOLD THE SHUTTLE"

Objective   The objective of all underhand shots, other than the serve, is to distract the opponent with deceptive moves. A phrase used often by badminton players, "holding the shuttle," refers to pretending to hit the shuttle before you actually do. For example, if when you pretend to play a dropshot, your opponent moves toward the net and you then flick the shuttle to the backcourt, you have "held the shot." This type of deception is generally employed with underhand shots. Deception on overhead shots results from preparing to stroke each shot identically as described in chapter two.

Procedure

1. You may hold the shot by a feint of the racket, head, or body. It takes time, however, to be deceptive.
2. If you are running at full speed to return the shuttle, there is not time to produce feints! When you find the pace is slower and you have the time, reach forward to play the shuttle; then let it drop and contact it at a lower point.
3. During the time the shuttle is dropping, your opponent may be committing himself forward or back. Be alert to this and either drop or flick the shuttle accordingly.
4. If your opponent is moving too soon and getting caught repeatedly, he will be forced to hold his position until you actually contact the shuttle.
5. Continue to watch the shuttle closely. You will tend to take your eye off the shuttle in order to see if and in which direction your opponent is moving.

If your errors tell you that you are mis-hitting and indulging in needless fancy racket work, go back to the basics. If you can master this deception, however, it is a tremendous weapon against a player who is very fleet of foot or likes to play a fast game. Slow the game down with defensive shots and then put your deception to work. Hopefully he will tire as a result; then you can apply your pace and power attack.

STROKES AND STRATEGY

Using the strokes described in chapters 2 and 3 in an appropriate sequence, you must outthink your opponent. Preconceived strategy and play are fine until you meet your equal or your supposed superior, in which case your thinking must be spontaneous. Your shots must have speed and control, and the decision as to the pattern or order they take must be made in the fury of the game. In singles, perhaps it will be two clears and then the drop, or clear and drop, and drop again; in doubles, a push shot, a smash, and another smash. In either game catch your opponent going the wrong way by not playing to the obvious open space; because he has moved to that obvious space, play behind him. Sometimes you may be caught in your own trap, but if your percentage of "catching" is greater than your percentage of being "caught," then you are ahead of the game.

If your strokes are well executed and the rallies are long and the play interesting and close, then consider your game successful. That's the fun of the game. Mastery of the strokes will make it possible for you to delight in meeting a contemporary and pitting your forces against his. Play with enthusiasm and enjoyment. The winning and the rewards, whatever they may be, will be forthcoming. Reaching this stage of enjoyment comes as a result of concentrated practice.

No amount of reading and thought off the court can substitute for hours of practice on the court. Both methods of learning, however, must be employed; therefore, the essentials of practicing will be discussed in the next chapter.

What is the prime factor determining your choice of shot while you are playing in the "up" position? How does the execution of a smash from this position differ from a smash taken from midcourt?

HOW TO PLAY MORE ADVANCED NET SHOTS

The Push Shot   The push shot is just what the name implies—a push, not a stroke. It is played at or above net level with the head of the racket up and the face of the racket flat. Its direction is angled downward. Refer to figure 3.1.

The use of the push shot, almost nonexistent in singles, becomes highly effective in doubles. When a doubles team takes an up-and-back formation, the shot should be pushed down with a medium amount of speed to the opponent's midcourt. This will place the shuttle just behind the net player and force the backcourt player to reach and stroke the shuttle up. Confusion often results as to which player should return this shot. Obviously, the push shot cannot be played from below net level.

The Smash   The other highly important net shot that has to be played above net level is the smash. The shot is accomplished by a downward snap of the wrist. It is the best return of a high, short shot. It is the kill! Care must be taken not to get excessively enthusiastic at the prospect of a setup and bang the shuttle or your racket into the net. Instead, keep your eye on the shuttle and control your swing until the point is completed. The direction of the smash at this close range is not important. If directed straight to the floor with great speed, the smash will be unreturnable. See figure 3.1.

progress can be speeded up

4

The first step in learning badminton, understanding the why and how of stroke development, must be followed by actual stroke practice. No amount of intellectual grasp of the game can substitute for either repetitive practice of the stroke pattern or coordination of the racket and shuttle to assure correct timing. Mental and physical processes should work together to speed up progress.

DRILLS AND SUGGESTIONS

Various drills and suggestions for the individual will be given in this chapter; group organization will be left to your instructor. In the diagrams that follow, — — — — — indicates path of the player. For successfully executed drills, locate another student with approximately the same degree of skill; neither player benefits sufficiently if the range of skill varies too greatly.

Overhead Clear Drill (fig. 4.1)   Both players take their center positions where the drill for the clear starts with a singles serve and thereafter continues with clears only. The clears should first be played parallel to the sideline, then crosscourt, then alternating straight and crosscourt, giving each player a chance to clear from both deep corners. The shuttle should be directed repeatedly to the same corner before changing the direction to the other corner. The player stroking from the backhand should be using an overhead or round-the-head clear. The object is to repeatedly clear the shuttle high and deep from one corner to an opposite corner between the doubles and singles back boundary line. Returning to center position after each hit develops good footwork and stamina.

   HINT: Get behind and in line with the shuttle for increased depth. Upon contact, step and move your weight towards the net.

Serve Drill   Perfecting the serve, which is one of the easiest strokes to practice, can be done with or without a partner. To permit the server to take his service position for twenty strokes before retrieving shuttles, about twenty shuttles should be collected. This not only saves time but also adds to the consistency of the stroke. The serve, whether for singles or doubles, should be directed to a particular corner on the court. Practice to all corners for singles and doubles. Even if a partner is present, the serve should not be returned; instead, it should be allowed to fall to the court, enabling the server to see exactly how close to the target the shuttle came.

HINT: Drop the shuttle well away from you in order to get the freedom of movement which will result in better accuracy.

Overhead Dropshot and Underhand Clear Drill (fig. 4.2)   Both players begin in the center position from which the drill starts with a singles serve by A to a back corner. The receiver B returns it with an overhead dropshot to a front corner. An underhand clear to the same back corner follows and the drill continues: drop, clear, drop, clear; until one player fails to return the shuttle. The shuttle should be directed repeatedly to the same corner until there is some degree of control before switching the direction of the shuttle to another front or back corner. Again, both players should return to the center position if the drill is to simulate game conditions.

HINT: Pretend to stroke an overhead clear and a hairpin net shot in order to acquire the deception needed for these two shots.

Smash and Underhand Clear Drill (fig. 4.3)   This drill, very much like the preceding drop and clear drill, begins with a singles serve by A to either back corner. The smash by B parallel to the sideline and to the opposite midcourt is returned with a high underhand clear. The drill then becomes—smash, clear, smash, clear; until either player misses; the drill then begins again from center with the serve.

HINT: Gradually increase the speed of your smash in order to eliminate faulty shots.

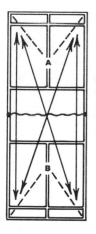

Fig. 4.1   Overhead clear drill

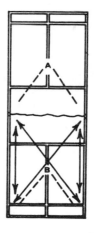

Fig. 4.2   Overhead dropshot and underhand clear drill

Drive Drill (fig. 4.4)   There are four drives to be practiced: the straight (parallel to the sideline) forehand and backhand, and the crosscourt forehand and backhand. This drill begins with both players in the center of the court. One player hits a driven serve to the predetermined forehand or backhand of the opponent. Thereafter, repeated drives ensue: forehand to forehand; backhand to backhand; forehand to backhand; and backhand to forehand. Each of the four strokes should be practiced repeatedly before the side and direction are changed. Return to center after each hit.

HINT: Contact the drive high so that this drill does not become a smash, clear drill.

Short Game (fig. 4.5)   This game, played and scored exactly according to singles rules, begins with a low serve by A and return of serve at the net by B: thereafter, only net shots, straight or crosscourt, can be played. Any shots, other than the serve, which fall behind the short service line are considered out of court. This drill, valuable to beginners learning rules and scoring, develops the skill and judgment in the forecourt necessary in doubles and mixed doubles.

HINT: Stand far enough away from the net to give yourself time and space to stroke properly.

CONDITIONING

Warm Up   It takes time to loosen up properly. Get off to a good, quick start on court by warming up sufficiently before going on court. Especially when playing competitively, you should increase your body temperature for maximum performance. Before going on court do the following:

1. Twist the trunk and do bending and squatting exercises.
2. Swing the racket while it is still in its cover or press, simulating the various badminton strokes, especially clears and drives.

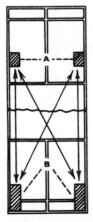

Fig. 4.3   Smash and underhand clear drill

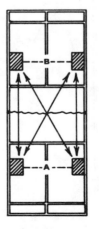

Fig. 4.4   Drive drill

3. Start slowly, gradually speeding up the swing.
4. Bounce on your feet to get your legs limber.
5. Practice quick starts with foot work similar to that on the court.
6. Take quick, short sprints—forward, backward, side to side, and diagonally.

MATCH PLAY CONDITIONING

Whether a player is able to finish the match or practice period in good fashion, that is, still stroking the shuttle with power and control, is determined largely by his physical condition. The player in poor condition begins to make errors and to be slow afoot after a short period of time. Badminton should be a game of long, interesting rallies free from outright errors, and this demands strength and endurance.

There are various ways of improving one's endurance. Distance running, hockey, basketball—in fact, all the running games—are of value. Modern dance, gymnastics, and rope skipping add quickness and flexibility. Tennis and squash racquets, closely related to badminton, provide stroke needs similar to the badminton player's game. All these activities contribute to the conditioning process, but obviously the best conditioning for badminton is to play badminton. If the stroke practice drills are rehearsed properly with each player returning to center position between each stroke, endurance will be developed. Practice games against someone of exact equal ability will result in long endurance-demanding rallies.

Needless to say, smoking and alcohol negatively affect one's physical condition. Adequate sleep and food supply the energy needed to meet the demands of a strenuous game.

Unequal Partner Drill   Many times good players unable to find opponents of like skill can devise ways of utilizing beginners as practice partners. For instance, the advanced player (A) strokes the shuttle to one corner of the court to the beginner (B) who may then return the shuttle any place on the court.

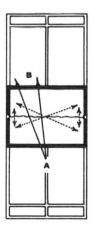

Fig. 4.5   Short game

Fig. 4.6   Unequal partner drill

The advanced player develops control by playing the shuttle to the beginner's racket, thus enabling him to keep the rally going. The advanced player develops footwork, stamina, and stroke control chasing the comparatively uncontrolled returns of the novice. This drill can be amusing and fun to two players desiring to learn (each at his own level) and willing to cooperate.

HINT: Enjoy the practice as if it were a game.

Three Stroke Drill   The first three strokes of a point, important because the offense or defense may easily be determined with initial strokes, should be practiced in that order and a decision made after each sequence as to the effectiveness of the serve, return of serve, and the third shot.

HINT: Try to be in an offensive position after the third stroke.

patterns of play

5

Certain tactics and strategy apply to all forms of badminton—singles, doubles or mixed doubles. Tactics are "skillful devices for accomplishing an end," a "mode of procedure for gaining advantage or success." In this chapter tactics or strategy of badminton are discussed in the following areas:

offense and defense
angle of return
crosscourt shots
receiving serves in singles
singles strategy
doubles strategy
mixed doubles strategy

OFFENSE AND DEFENSE

In offensive play, shots are directed downward. They are point winning shots such as smashes, half-smashes, dropshots, half-paced drives, and low serves. Winning a point from an overhead position requires speed, sharp angles and accurate direction. However, winning a point from an underhand stroke has to be accomplished through deception or superior court positioning.

In defensive play, shots are directed upward. These shots include the clear, underhand dropshots, drives and high serves. Offensive and defensive positions may change during the course of a rally. Defense can be changed to offense and vice versa, depending on how well a stroke is executed and selected for use at the proper time. For example, if you return a smash with an underhand hairpin net shot properly angled away from the smasher and the shot falls close to the net, the smasher is forced to hit up (defensive). If, however, the smash had been returned with an underhand clear or weak net shot, the offensive would have remained with the smasher.

Offensive players take chances and strive for outright winners, whereas defensive players are content to "play it safe" and wait for the opponent to err.

ANGLE OF RETURN

The angle of return, as important in badminton as it is in tennis, is the angle the returned shuttle takes in relation to the court boundaries. See figure 5.1. It does not refer to upward or downward angle.

To avoid being trapped by angle of return, position yourself on the court where the greater percentages of returns are likely to come. Occasionally you can neglect a portion of the court, a situation you strive for.

Examples: (See figure 5.1)

1. A high clear to your opponent's deep forehand or backhand corner can rarely be returned crosscourt high and deep to your diagonal corner because of the long distance. It could be returned with a flat, fast clear toward that corner, but you will be in the center blocking it before it reaches the intended spot.
2. A shot played to the center of the opponent's court will place the center of the angle of return on the centerline.

The best plan is to maintain your position in the center of the angle of possible returns and then be alert to the odd shot.

Winning badminton is generally a question of playing
basic fundamentals better than your opponent and
understanding and applying strategic principles.

CROSSCOURT SHOTS

Crosscourting and angle of return are closely related. Crosscourt shots travel a longer distance across the court and take more time to reach the intended spot than down-the-line shots. These shots travel a shorter distance and are more logical, but more obvious. For example, if you play the shuttle to your opponent's forehand side, anticipate the return on your backhand side. Your opponent can crosscourt to your forehand side, but the longer distance gives you more time to reach it.

Crosscourt when you are on balance and are able to return to center quickly and/or when the opponent has over anticipated.

1. A crosscourt shot of any kind played from forehand to forehand leaves the vulnerable backhand exposed.
2. Most of the time move about a foot to the side of the court to which you have directed the shuttle.
3. Move a step forward if your shot has forced your opponent to the baseline. He may be unable to get sufficient depth from your good length.

Try to trap your opponent by leading him into over anticipating certain shots because you have played crosscourt or down-the-line shots in a specific pattern. Then play the odd shot for a winner or to draw him away from a particular area. Many players leave the forehand side open and vulnerable in an effort to cover up a weak backhand.

Have a preconceived idea of how much you intend to use crosscourt shots and how to play each opponent. As the game progresses, both players will be trying various plans in hopes of achieving a successful one.

RECEIVING SERVE IN SINGLES

Ready Position   Your ready position for return of serve for singles and doubles is somewhat the same as ready position during a rally.

1. For receiving serve, place your feet comfortably apart with your left foot in advance of the right in a diagonal stance rather than parallel. This enables you to have an immediate push forward depending on whether it is a low or high deep serve.
2. It is imperative to move forward to smash a poor low serve or to move backward before the high serve gets behind you. Therefore, take your position to receive serve; place your feet in the diagonal stance and keep your feet stationary until the serve contacts the shuttle.

Receiving   It is important to anticipate the usual direction of the serves and to adjust your position accordingly, shifting your weight in that direction in order to get a faster start.

1. Do not over anticipate. If you do, the server is given the opportunity to surprise you with a change in direction or depth. Take care to keep your percentages in the proper balance.
2. Note in figure 5.2 that the receiver in the right service court is standing closer to the center line than to the sideline in order to protect his backhand side. The receiver in the left service court moves toward the backhand side for the same purpose.

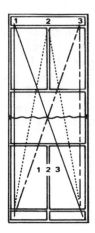

Fig. 5.1 Angle of return

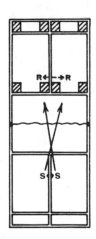

Fig. 5.2 Receiving serve in singles

3. In both cases the receiver is closer to the short service line than to the long service line. This position enables him to attack (hit down) the low serve if it appears. He has more time to move back for the high deep serve.

Common Faults in Receiving Serve

1. Standing too deep in the court, resulting in defensive (hitting up) return of the low serve.
2. Moving back too slowly letting the shuttle get behind the receiver.

Whether you are playing singles or doubles, the general rule to follow is to change your position if you are encountering difficulties. Find the place in the court and the position which best suits you and best defies your opponent's plans.

SINGLES STRATEGY

Singles can be described as a "running" game since it requires excellent physical condition to cover the 17 x 44 ft. area. Singles can be a difficult game for some players because it can expose weaknesses that might otherwise be covered up by a partner in doubles play.

The most effective shots in singles play are the high deep serve, the overhead clear, half-smash, underhand clear and the hairpin net return. Occasional shots used are the low serve, driven serve, drive, push shot and the full smash.

Serves   The high deep serve moves the opponent to the back boundary line and thus opens up the front of the court and moves the receiver out of center. The low serve used as a change of pace is a method of gaining the offensive since the shuttle may descend as shown as it reaches the top of the net. Therefore, it cannot be smashed downward.

Return of Serve   A clear to the opposite baseline is the best and safest return of a deep high serve. If the high serve is short you can dropshot, smash, half-smash, or use an attacking clear. The offensive can then be gained with an attacking shot. Choose the shot which you can execute effectively and deceptively.

As in the return of serve, shots during the rally which are short are disastrous. They can be dealt with more easily and with more variety than shots that fall perpendicular on the back boundary line.

Attack   In an offensive attack, remember the following:

1. Force your opponent to play a backhand from deep court.
2. Force your opponent to hit short by using good depth.
3. Hit to the forehand corner in order to open up the backhand side.
4. Meet the shuttle as soon as possible and give your opponent less time.

It is difficult to be deceptive unless you have plenty of time and are not struggling to reach the shuttle.

Defense   When the opportunity arises for your opponent to play a smash or a dropshot you must defend as well as possible. Play the shuttle close to the net or the baseline as midcourt shots have little value here. Try to use your opponent's speed or angle to your advantage by blocking or guiding the shuttle just over the net with a hairpin net shot. Direct the shuttle to the farthest distance from the attacker.

For example, if your opponent smashes or dropshots from the deep forehand corner, then you should hairpin net shot to the front backhand corner. If he anticipates the net shot and comes racing in toward the net, flick a flat clear to his backhand corner. Next time go ahead and play the net shot. Alternate your pattern so your opponent doesn't know what return to expect or just where to expect it.

Types of Singles Play

1. Fast and quick game shots include the low serve, driven serve, flat or attacking clear, drive, and smash.
2. Deliberate power game shots include the high serve, high clear, dropshot, and half-smash.

Many players are adept at both fashions of play and the use of a particular one depends on both the opponent and the situation.

DOUBLES STRATEGY

Doubles play, the most popular form of badminton, requires skill, wit, and cleverness. It is exciting, extremely fast, and demands excellent team work. It also requires less stamina than singles and is a game in which weaknesses can be disguised.

The most effective doubles serves include the low serve and driven serve. Other useful doubles shots are the drive, half-smash, smash and various net returns.

Through various maneuvers by the two partners, a player may not have to use his less adequate stroke. Instead, both players combine their best assets. Partners unequal in ability can work out a combination that is unusually stable and effective.

Four players, all of different skill levels, can combine and have great fun playing.

Serves   Whatever the system used, the serve is highly important as it gives the opportunity to score. In doubles, these are most often used: the low, the driven, and the flick. Of these, the low serve is the best.

Can you name several good choices for return of a high serve that is falling short?

Systems of Play   The three systems of doubles play are:

side-by-side (defensive)
up-and-back (attacking)
a combination of the two

Men's and ladies' doubles teams use all three systems. Mixed doubles teams prefer the up-and-back formation.

Side-by-Side or Defensive Formation (fig. 5.3)   A team in a sides formation (S and S) divides the court down the middle from net to back boundary line. Each player covers his half of the court, front and back. The basic serving and receiving positions for the team playing side-by-side place each player in the middle of his half of the court.

These positions, alterable as the situation changes, are defensive positions. The down-the-middle shots, those directed between the two players, are usually played by the player on the left side since this is his forehand side. A team with a left-handed player will discover some interesting advantages and disadvantages requiring some decisions. It could be agreed that the stronger player is to play the middle shots regardless of which is his forehand side.

The advantage of the sides system is that the area which each player is to defend is well defined and there is little confusion about who is to cover which shots. This defensive side formation is the best system when you have been forced to hit the shuttle upward, thus giving your opponents the opportunity to smash. With both players back from the net, they have more time to defend against the smash and to cover the areas (midcourt and backcourt) where a smash can be directed.

The disadvantage of the system is that the opposite team can play all the shots to one side, up and back, and tire one player. If one player is weaker than the other, the opponents will naturally launch their attack on him.

Up-and-Back or Offensive Formation (fig. 5.3)   In this system the court is divided in such a way that when a team is on the attack one player plays the forecourt (U) and the other player (B) plays the backcourt. Note the serving (S) and receiving (R & R) positions for this formation in figure 5.3. The dividing line is about midcourt, depending upon the agreement made by the two partners (P).

The advantage of the up-and-back system lies in the fact that there is always a player at the net to "put away" any loose returns. This keeps the pressure on the opponents.

For example, as soon as one player can smash or dropshot from the backcourt, his partner moves forward to the next position to cut off any weak returns. Crosscourt shots can be more easily blocked with a player at the net. In

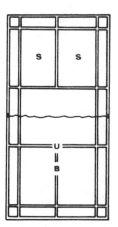

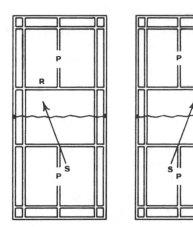

Fig. 5.3   Side-by-side and
up-and-back doubles formation

Fig. 5.4   Up-and-back doubles formation
serving to right and left courts

addition, this formation makes it easier to protect weaknesses, and for each player to cover the part of the court to which his game is best suited.

The disadvantage of the up-and-back system is that the midcourt area along the sidelines is vulnerable. The half-court shot that is played just behind the net player and just in front of the backcourt player tends to cause confusion as to which player is to hit the shuttle. The resulting slight delay may prove disastrous.

Which areas of the court are most vulnerable in the up-and-back formation? in the side-by-side formation?

Combination   The combination system is a means of rotating from up-and-back to side-by-side depending on whether a team is defending or attacking.

The aggressive team will have to relinquish the up-and-back formation when either player is forced to hit the shuttle upward (defensive). Therefore, when on defense, this team reverts to the side-by-side formation until it can regain the attack.

The up-and-back formation is an inadequate defense against the smash because the player at net will not have time to defend and his partner cannot protect the entire backcourt against a smash. The net player should backpedal quickly to either side, preferably the closer, and his partner adjusts accordingly.

Return of Serve   Any high serve should be returned with a smash or overhead dropshot, preferably the smash. However, most of the time the receiver will be low served and has a choice of returning with a drop, drive, or halfcourt. The *drop* should be deceptive, low, and played straight, not crosscourted. The *drive* return is used mostly and ideally has a flat trajectory, and when possible, it is directed to the backhand side although the direction should be varied when necessary. The *halfcourt* is the most difficult to execute as it has to be almost perfect like the drop return or it backfires. It should fall behind the net player at a downward angle in order to force the back player to hit up.

Offense   The primary object of the serve, return of serve, and succeeding shots is to force your opponents to hit up thereby giving your side the attack. When this objective is reached, the smash, the half-smash and overhead drop-shot come into play. The smash should win the point outright or force a weak return for the net man to "put away." When smashing, it is very important to be on balance and for the smash to have a sharp downward angle. It should be played to the inside of the opponent who is straight ahead of you. Crosscourt smash only for variety and to keep both opponents alert. The half-smash is extremely useful to change the pace particularly after full paced smashes have been used. Overhead dropshots will take less effort and therefore they have their merits. Indiscriminate and nonpurposeful smashing is not intelligent. Mix the overhead drop, smash, and half-smash judiciously and the rewards will be obvious.

Defense   Despite all efforts to keep the shuttle going down to maintain the offense, at times your opponents will force you to defend. How good or how bad your opponents are will determine the amount of time you spend defending your court! The smash and dropshot can be returned with a high deep clear, or if possible and ideally with a flatter shot at head or shoulder level. The high deep clear keeps you on defense only with the hope of an error by the smasher. The half-clear or drive return initiates the turn from defense to offense.

MIXED DOUBLES STRATEGY

Mixed doubles, played by men and women in the up-and-back formation, is a great attacking game and probably the one played most often at the club or in the backyard. It is superior to many games involving men and women because it is impossible for the man to concentrate his attack on the opposing woman with any degree of success. A more well-balanced game results in badminton than in tennis because the badminton net is at a five foot height and the court is relatively small. For example, if the opposing man decides to smash the shuttle at the woman, she merely ducks below net level and lets the shuttle pass on for her partner to play. Because the court is not very wide, the man can cover it effectively.

See figures 5.5 and 5.6 for serving and receiving positions.

Duties of the Woman Player

1. Plays shots in the front court and around the short service line.
2. Tries to control the attack by directing the shuttle downwards.
3. Uses net and half court shots to direct shuttle downward.
4. Smashes any "loose" (high and short) shots.

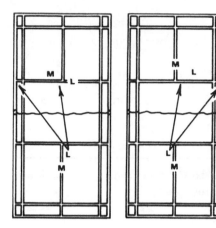
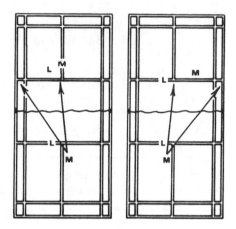

Fig. 5.5 Mixed doubles formation— lady serving

Fig. 5.6 Mixed doubles formation— man serving

5. Lets clears, fast drives and smashes pass her to be played by her partner.
6. Rarely moves to the backcourt to play.

Duties of the Man Player

1. Plays shots behind and around short service line.
2. Plays half-court shots, drives and smashes.
3. Plays downward shots that will force a weak return for his partner to "put away."

Use of the Low Serve

1. Keep it low-controlled to inside corner (less angle).
2. Serve to the outside corner to keep the receiver off balance.
3. Flick serve keeps the receiver off balance and from constantly rushing the low serve.
4. High serve to the woman if she is slow moving back or has limited strength overhead.

Return of Serve

1. The halfcourt shot is the safest and most used. It has moderate speed, falls behind the woman at a downward angle, forcing the man to hit up. Play the halfcourt straight rather than crosscourt most of the time.
2. The dropshot is best used when the woman is serving and should be placed in the alley farthest from her. It is risky to dropshot the man's serve as the woman's position is too far from the net in anticipation of a halfcourt.
3. The drive is pushed or punched faster than the halfcourt and deep in the court. Sometimes a punch directly at the man cramps him and narrows his angle of return as well.

Strategy

1. Use the dropshot and halfcourt to keep the opposing woman guessing and off balance.
2. Use the half court and drive against the opposing man. These shots are best and safest since they are not hit up and they are intended to force an upward return. An upward return is replied with by a smash. Smashes win points.
3. Avoid lifting or hitting the shuttle up.

Normally, the woman plays up in the mixed doubles game. Do you know when it is advisable for her to drop back a few feet?

The rallies often generate into driving duels between two men with the better driver winning. If you concede that your opponent is excellent at driving, then make more use of the halfcourt and perhaps the drop if the woman is less effective than her partner. It is important for the man to use good judgment when electing to crosscourt a drive by being cognizant of his center position.

Special Defensive Position   Occasions will arise when you will be forced to hit up and defend against a smash. Usually the woman should back up several feet and defend against the crosscourt smash. The man is then responsible for the down-the-line smash and for the dropshot played straight. This net area has now become vulnerable since the woman has backed out and to one side in an effort to return the crosscourt smash.

Conclusion

1. Direct the play to your strengths and to your opponent's weaknesses.
2. Play to your partner's best abilities, cooperate, and discuss your plans.
3. Enjoy the game.

Partners do not enjoy each other if they feel they are not getting to play their own or best shots. The man should not play shots better played by the woman. The woman should play shots that will be dealt with by the man's strengths.

the language and lore of badminton

6

Modern sports often have peculiar, albeit fascinating sounding terms. Pursuing the origins of the language of individual sports would doubtlessly provide many hours of interesting research.

For example, what explains the "side" of badminton's "side in," "side out," when there are never more than two players on one side of the net? A bit of investigation reveals that in its early years the game was played by sides consisting of at least three players, and usually four or five! Singles and doubles were nonexistent. Instead, a team consisted of several players who served in turn until they were individually eliminated. When all team members had finished serving, thus completing an inning, that group was said to be "side out." Currently the term "service over" is used in the official rules but players continue to say "side out."

Although singles and doubles are the accepted events in competition today, there are still countries, the majority Asian, where the many-sided game is still popular because of a surplus of badminton players, a lack of available courts, and a lust for long rallies which are, of course, prolonged because every inch of the court is covered by someone!

The derivations of the terms presented in the following glossary are equally fascinating, and pursuit of them by the curious student would promise interesting results. Some of them have been more fully described in earlier chapters of this book.

Alley. Extension of the court by 1½ ft. on both sides for doubles play. Referred to by the English as "tramline."

Back Alley. Area between back boundary and long service lines.

Badminton. The game we know today derived its name from the village of Badminton in Gloucestershire. It was here in the early 1860s at the Duke of Beaufort's estate that this new game, which was brought back from India by some Army officers, was first played in England.

Balk. Any deceptive movement which disconcerts an opponent before or during service. Often called a "feint."

Bird. The object with feathers which flies through the air over a badminton court in place of a ball. Parrot and eagle "birds" are popular in Thailand, bluebirds in Denmark. Officially known as shuttlecock. Commonly referred to as shuttle (fig. 1.1).

Block. Placing the racket in front of the shuttle and letting it rebound into the opponent's side of the court. Not a stroke.

Carry. Momentarily holding the shuttle on the racket during the execution of a stroke. Also called a sling or a throw. This is an illegal procedure.

Center or Basic Position. Position in which a player stands in relation to the lines of the court, the net, the opponent, and the shuttle.

Clear. High, deep shot hit to the back boundary line (figs. 2.8 and 3.4).

Combination Doubles Formation. Rotation of the side-by-side and the up-and-back formations (fig. 5.3).

Court. Area of play. The area bounded by the outer lines of play has not always had the same shape, and the dimensions have, therefore, also differed. Although rules and regulations were drawn up as early as 1877 by Colonel H. O. Selby, Royal Engineers, and published in book form in Karachi, West Pakistan (then a part of India), the numerous different interpretations with reference to the size and shape of the court unfortunately delayed the development of the game. In the early part of the century in India the court was actually laid out on a ground about the size of a lawn tennis court, 78 ft. by 36 ft., and up to five persons played on each side (no wonder!). In England this confusion can be traced to the 1860s when the Duke of Beaufort introduced this glorified form of battledore and shuttlecock to his guests. The room in which the game was played had two large doors openings inwards on the side walls. In order to allow nonplaying guests to enter and leave the room without disturbing the game in progress, it was decided to narrow the court considerably at the net, thus originating the "hour-glass" shaped court. Variations of this peculiarly shaped court were maintained for thirty years, and the first three All-England Championships actually took place under these trying conditions. Even in 1911 two English clubs, playing home and away team matches, found themselves playing first on a court 60 ft. by 30 ft., then on one 44 ft. by 20 ft.!

Crosscourt Shots. Shots hit diagonally from one side of the court to the other.

Deception. The art of deceiving or outwitting one's opponent. Accomplished in badminton with deceptive stroking by changing the direction and speed of the shuttle at the last minute.

Double Hit. Hitting the shuttle twice in succession on the same stroke. An illegal procedure.

Drive. A fast and low shot which makes a horizontal flight pattern over the net (figs. 2.13 and 2.15).

Driven Serve. Quickly hit serve having a flat trajectory (fig. 2.4).

Dropshot. Finesse stroke hit with very little speed which falls close to the net on the opponent's side (fig. 2.10). In Malaysia the slowest type of drop is called the Coconut Drop because it falls perpendicularly. Described in this book as the hairpin net shot (fig. 2.4).

Ends of Court. Refers to the physical boundaries of the court on either side of the net.

Fault. Any violation of the rules. Most faults are broadly classified as either serving or receiving faults, or faults occurring "in play."

First Service. Normally used in doubles. Denotes that the player serving retains service.

Flat. The flight of the shuttle with a level horizontal trajectory. Also, the angle of the face of the racket which does not impart spin to the shuttle.

Flick. Speeding up the shuttle with a quick wrist action. Useful in stroking from below the level of the net, thereby surprising an opponent by quickly changing a soft shot into a faster passing shot.

Game. A game unit consists of fifteen points in men's singles and in all doubles games; eleven points constitutes a game in ladies' singles. See "Setting."

Game Bird. Game winning point.

Hairpin Net Shot. Stroke made from below and very close to the net with the shuttle just clearing the net and then dropping sharply downward. Takes its name, hairpin, from the shape of the shuttle's flight in a perfectly executed shot (fig. 2.4).

Halfcourt Shot. Shot placed midcourt. Used more in doubles than in singles play, especially against the up-and-back formation (fig. 2.7).

Hand. An outdated term meaning service. First Hand and Second Hand are now correctly called First Service and Second Service.

IBF. International Badminton Federation. The world governing body established in July, 1934, at which time badminton had become sufficiently worldwide in its appeal to warrant international organization. The IBF is governed by an annual meeting of the elected representatives of every national association included in its membership. One of its many functions is the management of the world famous international team competitions for the Thomas Cup and the Uber Cup.

Inning. Term of service. Time during which a player or side holds the service.

In Play. The shuttle is said to be "in play" from the time it is struck by the server's racket until it touches the ground or a fault or let occurs. See exception in Laws (chap. 7).

"In" Side. Player or team having the right to serve.

Kill. Fast downward shot which usually cannot be returned. A putaway.

Let. Legitimate cessation of play to allow an exchange or rally to be replayed.

Love. No score. English pronunciation of the French word "l'œuf" meaning goose-egg or zero. To start a singles match the umpire calls "Love-All, Play." To start a doubles match he says "Hand Out, Love-All, Play."

Love-All. No score. Also used after a game has been set. See "setting."

Match. Best two out of three games.

Match Point. Match-winning point.

Net Shot. Shot hit from the forecourt with the shuttle just clearing the netcord. Hairpin net shots, push shots, and net smashes are the three most popular net shots (fig. 2.4).

New York Badminton Club. Founded in 1878, the NYBC claims to be the oldest organized club in the world, although until the early part of this century it was more a club of social prominence than a center designed for badminton activity.

No Shot. Badminton etiquette requires a player to immediately call "no shot" when he has faulted by carrying, slinging, or throwing the shuttle.

"Out" Side. Side receiving serve: opposite of "in" side.

Point. Smallest unit in scoring.

Poona. Some historians believe the original name for badminton was "poona," the name coming from the city of Poona in India where a badminton-type game was played in the 1860s.

Push Shot. A gentle net shot played by merely pushing the shuttle without force (fig. 3.1).

Ready Position. An alert body position enabling the player to make quick movement in any direction (fig. 2.3).

Round-the-Head Shot. Stroke peculiar to badminton. An overhead stroke played on the left side of the body. The contact point is above the left shoulder (fig. 3.6).

Rush the Serve. Quick spurt to the net in an attempt to put away a low serve simply by smashing the shuttle down into an opponent's court. Used mostly in doubles.

Second Service. Normally used in doubles. Indicates that one partner is "down," i.e., he has already had his turn at serving.

Serve or Service. Act of putting the shuttle into play. Opening stroke of each exchange or rally (fig. 2.5).

Service Court. Area into which serve must be delivered, determined by the score.

Setting. Method of extending games by increasing the number of points necessary to win tied games. Player reaching tied score first has option of setting. Further described in chapter 7.

Set Up. Poor shot which makes a "kill" easy for the opponent.

Shuttlecock (fig. 1.1). Official name for shuttle or "bird." The traditional shuttlecock, made with precious goose feathers and described in chapter 1, is still used officially in all major competitions today. The first synthetic shuttle was made from plastic. More recently, nylon shuttles represent a considerable improvement over the plastic ones, and are popular in less important tournaments as well as in club matches. Shuttles have varied over the years. Early tournament players often had their choice between a "rocket" and a "slow wobbler." They continued playing with one shuttle until it lost several feathers as well as its original shape. Those used in the first few All-England Championships were called barrel shuttles because of their shape. In early years unsuccessful efforts were made to produce fabric and papier-mache shuttles. India tried making a substitute ball of Berlin wool wound on a double disc of cardboard 2½ in. in diameter with a central hole of 1 in., but it flew too fast.

Side-by-Side. A doubles formation (fig. 5.3).

Side-In and Side-Out. See beginning of this chapter.

Smash. Hard hit overhead shot which forces the shuttle sharply downward. The game's chief attacking stroke (fig. 3.2).

Stroke. Action of striking the shuttle with the racket.

Do you know the meaning of the following terms: block, game bird, no shot, wood shot?

Toss. Before play begins, opponents toss a coin or spin a racket, and the player winning the toss or spin has a choice of serving, receiving, or making a choice of sides.

USBA. United States Badminton Association. The national governing body in the United States was founded in 1936, then known as American Badminton Association.

Up-and-Back. Popular doubles and mixed doubles formation (figs. 5.5 and 5.6).

Wood Shot. The shot which results when the base of the shuttle is hit by the frame of the racket rather than by the strings. Although they have not always been legal, the IBF ruled in 1963 that wood shots were acceptable.

laws of the game
7

The International Badminton Federation together with the United States Badminton Association annually publishes a handbook containing the rules of badminton, officially termed "laws," as well as interpretations and revisions of these laws. Although an official handbook should be consulted for any tournament play, the following set of rules will suffice for scholastic and recreational play. The IBF has established laws pertinent to the court, equipment, players, toss, method of scoring, etc. These laws change from time to time. Both organizations should be consulted for tournament play. (Addresses are in chapter 9.)

Playing Surface and Equipment

1. The singles court measures 17 ft. wide and 44 ft. long; the doubles court measures 20 ft. wide and 44 ft. long. See figures 1.2 and 1.3 in chapter 1.
2. A net 5 ft. 1 in. in height bisects the court; the net posts are placed on the doubles sideline. The net dips in the center to a height of exactly 5 ft.
3. A detailed description of the official present-day shuttle will be found in the section on equipment. In order to insure the game's taking the same form whenever and wherever it is played, it is imperative to standardize a shuttle's speed. A profound difference in the type of game results if a fast shuttle instead of a slow shuttle is selected for use. The heavier the shuttle, the faster it flies. Each grain adds about four inches in length to its flight. The shuttle also flies faster under conditions of increased temperature and altitude. Weights of manufactured shuttles therefore vary from 73 to 85 grains in order to meet conditions at a particular time. Under normal conditions a 79- or 80-grain shuttle should be used. Each time the game is played the shuttle should function at the same speed regardless of atmospheric conditions. The testing of a shuttle's speed takes place just before matches are to begin.

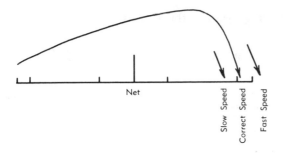

Fig. 7.1   Shuttle test

The test is made by having a player of average strength strike the shuttle with a full underhand stroke from a spot immediately above the back boundary line in a line parallel to the sidelines and at an upward angle. It is deemed correctly paced if it falls not less than 1 ft. or more than 2 ft. 6 in. short of the other back boundary line (see fig. 7.1).

Players

4.   Players are those persons taking part in the game: one player on a side in singles, two players on a side in doubles. The side which has the serve is called the "in" side and the opposing side, the "out" side.

Toss

5.   Before play begins, the opposing sides shall toss a coin or a racket. The winner of the toss shall have the option of serving first, not serving first, or choosing ends of the court. The side losing the toss shall then have a choice of the remaining alternatives. Decisions made at this time can be very important. One end of the court may be more desirable than the other because of lighting arrangements, floor conditions, and location of spectators. Outdoors, the wind and sun are major factors.

Scoring

6.   Play is started by an underhand serve, and a side can score only when serving (fig. 7.2). Each time an exchange or rally is won while serving, one point is recorded. If the exchange is lost while serving, neither side is awarded a point. Instead, the right to serve is relinquished and the opposing side then has the chance to serve and score.

7.   Doubles and men's singles games consist of 15 points; ladies' singles, 11 points. Peculiar to the scoring system is the term "setting." This is a

method of extending the length of a game if the game is tied at a particular score. See the chart below.

Points in Game	Score Set At	Points Required to Win Game
11	9 all	3 points
11	10 all	2 points
15	13 all	5 points
15	14 all	3 points

The side which reached the tied score first has the option of setting or not setting the score. If the side elects not to set the score, then the conventional number of points completes the game. A side which did not set the score at the first opportunity may have the opportunity, however, to set the score should the occasion arise again. In doubles, for example, if the score is tied at 13 all, and the team that reached 13 first declared no set, then play continues to 15. If, however, the score becomes tied at 14 all, whichever team reached 14 first is offered the opportunity to set the score.

8. A match shall consist of the best of three games. The players change ends at the beginning of the second game and at the beginning of the third game, if a third game is necessary to decide the match. In the third game, players shall change sides when either player first reaches 8 in a game of 15 points and 6 in a game of 11 points. The object of this change of ends is to try to give both players equal time on both ends of the court. If players forget to change ends, they shall change as soon as their mistake is discovered.

9. An inning indicates a term of service and there may be any number of innings since many rallies are played for which no points are scored.

10. In doubles, each player on a team of two players is referred to as a server while serving his inning. First service is when the initial player is serving. Second service is when the other player serves. Service over occurs when both servers lose their serves. The side or team beginning a game has only one turn at serving in its first inning. Thereafter, both players on a side have a turn and both players take their turn in the innings.

When the score is tied at 13-all, which team has the option of setting? If the team elects not to set and the score then becomes tied at 14-all, what happens?

Playing the Game

11. If a player attempting a serve misses the shuttle completely, he may re-stroke. An infinite number of attempts may be made provided the racket does not touch any part of the shuttle.

12. A serve is deemed completed as soon as the shuttle is struck by the server's racket. Unlike the serve in tennis, only one serve is allowed a player to put the shuttle into play.

13. After the serve is completed, players on both sides may take any positions they wish irrespective of boundaries.

14. A shot falling inside the boundaries or directly on a line is considered good.

15. In singles, players serve from and receive in the right service court when the server's score is zero or an even number. When the server's score is an odd number of points, players serve from and receive in the left service court.

16. In doubles, when their score is an even number, partners should be in the courts (right or left service court) in which they began the game. When the team's score is an odd number, then their court positions should be reversed.

17. The player or team that wins a game always serves first in the next game. At this point, in doubles, a team's serving order may be changed. For example, the losing team might decide that it could be more successful if a different player served first.

18. When any unusual occurrence interferes with the play, a "let" (replay of the point) can be invoked. This happens, for example, if a stray shuttle from a nearby court interferes, or if a linesman and umpire are unable to make a decision on a particular shot.

The IBF has also some established laws (adopted by the USBA) which cannot be violated without penalty. If any violation of the following laws occur, it is either point or side-out. In other words, if the receiving side errs, the serving side scores a point; if the serving side breaks a rule, no point is scored but it becomes service over and the opponents then serve.

Faults During Serving and Receiving

19. A serve must be an underhand stroke and the shuttle must be contacted below the server's waist. To further insure that the serve is an underhand stroke, the shaft of the racket must point downwards and the entire head of the racket must be discernibly below the hand and fingers holding the racket. See figure 2.5, and figure 7.2.

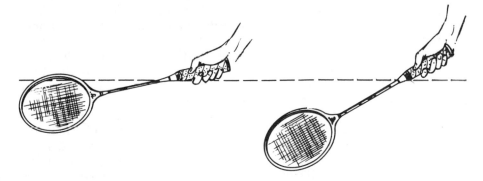

Fig. 7.2   Illegal serve, legal serve

20. A player's feet must be stationary and in their correct count upon delivery of the serve. It is not a fault if a server takes up his stance and then takes one step forward, provided he has not started to swing his racket before completing the step.

21. The server should not serve until the receiver is ready. If the receiver attempts to return the serve, however, he is judged ready. If a player is not ready, he should let the shuttle fall to the court and then tell the server or the umpire that he was not ready, in which case the serve shall be delivered again. This rule keeps the player who has a tendency to hurry his opponent from gaining an undue advantage.

22. No preliminary feints or movements to distract the receiver once the service has started are allowed. The first forward movement of the server's racket constitutes the start of the service. A preliminary feint is any movement by the server that has the effect of breaking the continuity of the serve after the two players have taken their ready positions to begin the point. Such action is termed a balk, and a balk is a fault. It is also a fault if the server delays hitting the shuttle for so long as to be unfair to the receiver.

23. A serve that lands outside the boundaries of the service court is a fault.

24. A player may not serve out of turn or from the wrong court, and the receiver may not be in the wrong court. The consequences of an infraction of this rule depend upon when the mistake is discovered. If the player who commits one of these serving or receiving errors wins the rally, and the mistake is then discovered, a let is called. If the player at fault loses the rally, the mistake stands, that is, no let. If the mistake is not discovered before the next point commences, the already altered serving and receiving order is not changed until the end of the game regardless of which team won or lost the rally.

25. A serve may not be received twice in succession in an inning by the same player in doubles. If this occurs and points are scored, the error stands and the next serve is delivered to the other player.

26. The receiver's partner may not strike a serve meant for his partner.

27. If the shuttle falls outside the boundaries, passes through or under the net, fails to pass the net, touches the roof or side walls, or touches a person or the dress of a person, the rally ceases and the player committing the fault is penalized. However, a serve hitting the top of the net and going into the correct service court is legal and "in play." Some gymnasiums or halls may have low beams, ropes, or other obstructions hanging over the court. In such cases the local association may establish a ground rule to the effect that a shuttle hitting the obstruction would not be considered a fault, but a let. If careful judgment by an experienced person is not made in this case, a player might intentionally hit the obstruction when it appeared that he was going to lose the point. If an obstruction can be hit deliberately, the fault rule is usually enforced. An unusual and uncommon situation develops when a shuttle passes the net outside of the net post and then flies into the court. This is the only case in which the shuttle can go below the

net level and still be legal. It is most likely to occur outside on a windy day.

28. A player may not reach over the net to contact a shuttle. He may, however, contact the shuttle on his side of the net and follow through with his racket on the opponent's side, providing the net is not touched.

29. When the shuttle is "in play" a player may not touch the net or the net posts with his body, his racket, or his clothing. If he should hit the net following a stroke and after his shot has struck the floor, a fault does not result because the shuttle is not "in play" after it strikes the floor.

30. The shuttle may not be hit twice in succession before being returned to the opponent. This rule prevents setting the shuttle up to oneself or to one's partner.

31. The shuttle may not rest momentarily on the racket during the execution of the stroke. Commonly called "carry," "sling," or "throw," it is difficult to detect this fault, and it is often committed unintentionally by beginners because of poor timing. More advanced players seldom commit this fault outright, but occasionally when a deceptive technique is attempted the infraction may occur. When a "carry" is committed, the shuttle's speed and direction are changed. This naturally handicaps the receiver of such a shot, and a player should not be penalized by another player's poor technique. The rule, then, is an essential one, and any player at fault should immediately call "No Shot."

32. A fault is called when a player is hit by the shuttle whether he is standing inside or outside the court boundaries. It is surprising to many players to realize that if they are able to hit their opponent with the shuttle, the point is theirs! This, however, is more difficult to accomplish than it sounds.

33. If a shuttle is hit into the net or caught in the net on the striker's side, it is not "in play." If the shuttle goes over the net, a let results. The point is replayed since the player on whose side the shuttle was caught did not have a fair chance of returning the shuttle. If the player attempted to play the shuttle that was caught in the net and in doing so hit the net, then a "fault," rather than a let, would be called.

34. A player may not step on his opponent's side of the net even when, in returning a close net shot, he cannot stop his momentum until his feet are in his opponent's court.

35. A player may not bend down below the net and intentionally hold his racket above the net hoping that the shuttle will happen to rebound from his racket into the opponent's court. This occasionally happens when a player close to the net tries to defend against a smash. On the other hand, a racket held in front of a player's face for protection is a good maneuver and any resulting shot is acceptable.

36. A player may not "unsight" another player. This rule, applicable only in doubles, means that the server's partner cannot stand in front of the server in such a way that the receiver cannot see the shuttle about to be served.

If this situation occurs, the receiver tells the server or the umpire, before the shuttle is served, that he cannot see the shuttle. An adjustment of the starting positions is then made by the serving side.

Disqualification

37. Play must be continuous. A player violating this rule is not just faulted, he is disqualified. A player therefore may not leave the court, receive advice, or rest at any time from the start to the conclusion of the match. The umpire shall judge whether this rule has been broken and shall disqualify any offenders. Certain countries, where climatic conditions make it desirable, allow a five-minute rest period between the second and third games. In the United States a five-minute rest interval is allowed in all matches.

A thorough and accurate knowledge of the rules makes for a smooth, pleasurable game. Many misunderstandings can be avoided by the player who knows not only the rules but the reasons for them.

UNWRITTEN RULES

Badminton, like all sports, has unwritten as well as written rules. The etiquette of badminton commences with your first introduction to the game.

Clothing   Wear clean, white, comfortable clothing. Clean socks are especially important for healthy feet. For sensitive feet, two pairs of socks are recommended.

Club Play

1. Attend club meetings regularly and pay your dues promptly.
2. Help with setting up equipment.
3. Be fair in contributing a fair share of shuttlecocks.
4. Be on time for practice.

Conduct on the Court

1. Call faults on yourself promptly and fairly.
2. Make line decisions correctly.
3. Do not ask spectators to help with decisions.
4. Avoid suggesting replays repeatedly.
5. If you are serving, call the score before each point.
6. Avoid abusive language and racket throwing.

Tournament Play

Before the Match:

1. Fill out entry blank accurately and completely and return the entry blank on time.

2. Report to the committee immediately upon arrival at the tournament. Find out your opponent's name, time of match, and court number.
3. Avoid being late for your match necessitating a default. Fifteen minutes is the time limit.

During the warm up:

1. Agree on a correct shuttle for use.
2. Hit the shuttle to your opponent so he also can warm up.

During the match:

1. Be sure your opponent is ready before you serve.
2. Retrieve shuttles on your side of the net and those nearest you. After a point, return the shuttle to your opponent to serve, not just over the net.
3. Ask your opponent first if you wish to change shuttles.
4. Play your best even if your opponent does not have your expertise. It is insulting to your opponent to do otherwise.

Following the match:

1. Shake hands and thank your opponent and the umpire.
2. Report the score to official table and find out the time of your next match.

After the tournament:

1. Write a thank you note to the tournament chairman and to the hostess or school if you have received complimentary housing.

In all competitive play, learning to win and lose gracefully is essential. Don't blame your defeat on some trivial matter or excuse for poor play. Keep your thoughts to yourself, analyze your play and determine to increase your abilities.

OFFICIATING

The officials needed to conduct a match are an umpire, one or two service judges and ten linesmen. National, international and world championship matches require this full complement of officials. Locally, twelve or thirteen officials are rarely available until the final round. State and school matches are often played without any officials whatsoever, in which case the players themselves keep score and conduct the match.

Duties of the Officials   The umpire conducts the match, calls the score and enforces the laws of badminton. The service judge rules on illegal serves (Rules 20 and 22), service faults (Rule 19), and on receiving faults (Rule 20). The linesmen determine if the shuttle is inside or outside the line. If the service judges or linesmen cannot make a decision, they may ask the umpire to do so.

For those particularly interested in this facet of the game, information can be found in the *USBA Rule Book* or the *IBF Handbook*. See Selected References.

The following illustration shows the position of officials for a match. U refers to the umpire, SJ to the service judge, and L to linesmen.

L   L   L   Fig. 7.3   Location of officials on court

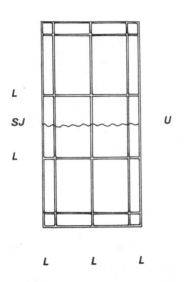

Conduct of the Match

1. Only an official has the privilege of communicating with players. The one exception is during the intermission that comes at the end of the second game if a third game is required to determine the winner of the match.
2. Applause between points is welcomed but there should be complete silence while the shuttle is in play.
3. Decisions of the linesmen are final and, in their absence, the umpire in charge will ask if he wishes help at any time on line decisions.

Following is a sample scoresheet used by the umpire.

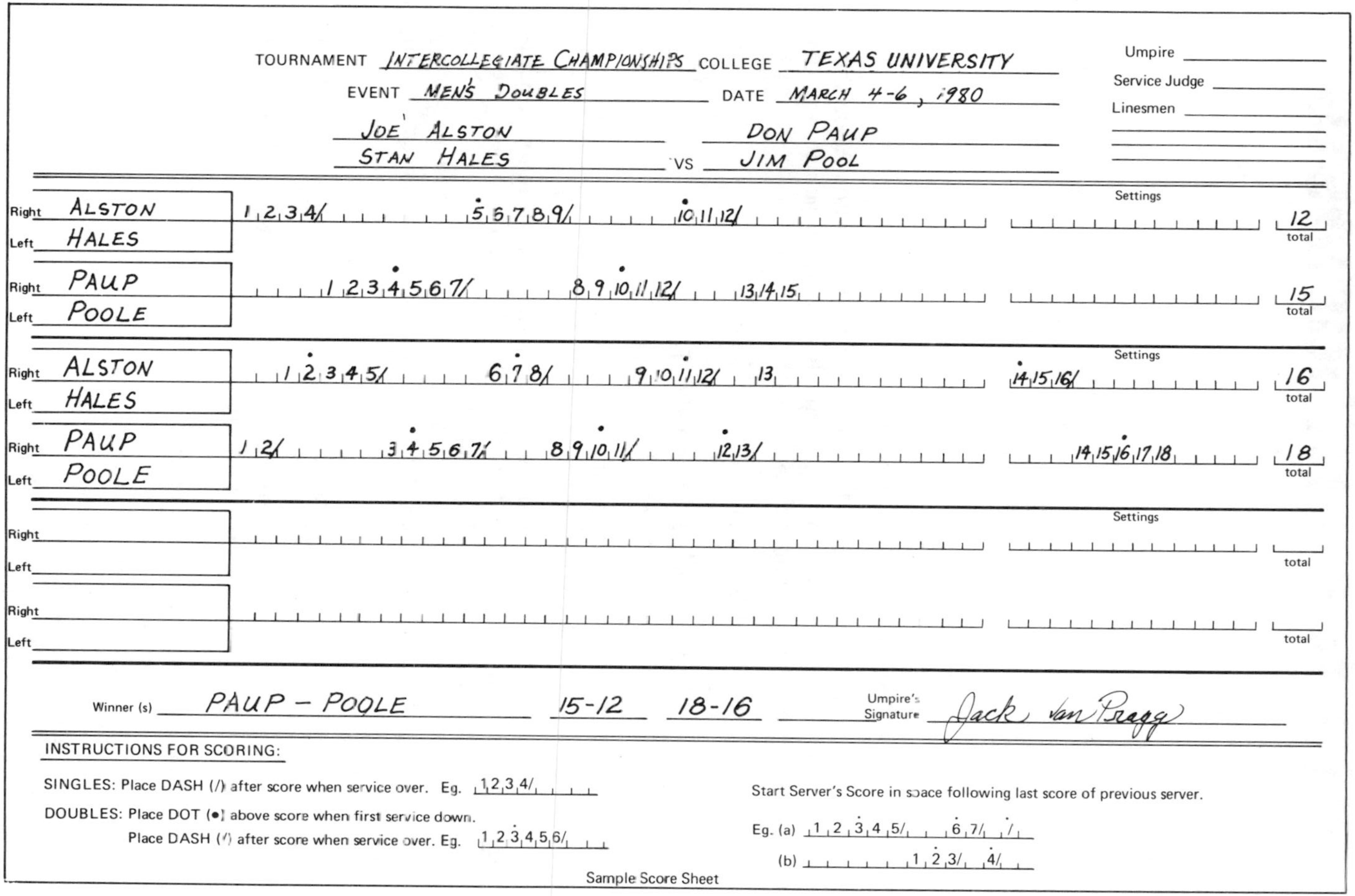

TOURNAMENT _INTERCOLLEGIATE CHAMPIONSHIPS_ COLLEGE _TEXAS UNIVERSITY_

EVENT _MEN'S DOUBLES_   DATE _MARCH 4-6, 1980_

JOE ALSTON   DON PAUP
STAN HALES _vs_ JIM POOL

Umpire _____
Service Judge _____
Linesmen _____

Right	Left

Right ALSTON   1, 2, 3, 4/   5, 6, 7, 8, 9/   •10, 11, 12/
Left HALES

Settings |12| total

Right PAUP   1, 2, 3, 4, •5, 6, 7/   •8, 9, 10, 11, 12/   13, 14, 15,
Left POOLE

Settings |15| total

Right ALSTON   1, •2, 3, 4, 5/   6, •7, 8/   •9, 10, 11, 12/   13,
Left HALES

Settings |14, 15, 16/| |16| total

Right PAUP   1, 2/   3, •4, 5, 6, 7/   8, •9, 10, 11/   12, 13/
Left POOLE

Settings |14, •15, 16, 17, 18| |18| total

Right _____
Left _____

Settings | | total

Right _____
Left _____

| | total

Winner (s) __PAUP - POOLE____15-12____18-16__

Umpire's Signature _Jack van Benge_

INSTRUCTIONS FOR SCORING:

SINGLES: Place DASH (/) after score when service over. Eg. 1,2,3,4/

DOUBLES: Place DOT (•) above score when first service down.   Start Server's Score in space following last score of previous server.

Place DASH (/) after score when service over. Eg. 1,2,3,4,5,6/   Eg. (a) 1, 2, 3, 4, 5/   •6, 7/, •/

(b) 1, 2, 3/, •4/

Sample Score Sheet

Fig. 7.4   Sample scoresheet

facts for enthusiasts
8

UNITED STATES BADMINTON ASSOCIATION

The governing body for badminton is the United States Badminton Association (USBA). It governs six regions, which in turn administers the activities of the state associations and their member clubs.

> United States Badminton Association
> P. O. Box 237
> Swartz Creek, Michigan 48473
> Telephone: (313) 655-4502

This organization is well worth your support because it serves the badminton player in many respects. Its purposes include:

1. Promotion of national and international competition in badminton without monetary gain; promotion and development of the game.
2. Establishment and upholding of rules of play.
3. Arranging and managing national tournaments in the United States.
4. Sanctioning of regional, sectional, state, city and other local tournaments in the United States.
5. Acting as U.S. authority in any international tournaments.
6. Choosing and managing of teams representing the U.S. in international competition.
7. Representation of U.S. interests in international badminton decisions and activities of the International Badminton Federation.

Other services, and there are too many to reprint here, include "approval" at no charge of high school, college and university activities. Detailed information is available from the national office.

Although USBA does not sell equipment, it will help locate suppliers if you have a particular problem.

One of USBA's most important functions is its responsibility for establishing the rules under which badminton is played in the United States. It therefore publishes the "Official Rules of Play," available from the national office at a very nominal price.

Inquiries to the USBA office should be directed to Mr. Cletus Eli, the Secretary-Treasurer.

To keep up with badminton national rankings, tournament schedules and results, the official USBA magazine, *Badminton USA*, is published five times per year. Edited by Brian Bretzke, it also includes articles of interest to both club and tournament player in the United States, and costs only $5 yearly.

> Brian Bretzke, Editor
> *Badminton USA*
> P.O. Box 237
> Swartz Creek, Michigan 48473
> Telephone: (313) 655-4502

An attractive blue and white pamphlet available upon request gives more information on USBA. You are encouraged to join or to at least become a "subscriber member" by subscribing to *Badminton USA*.

Five other memberships are available: Life, regular, 22 and under, club and institution. Life membership is granted to those making a one-time contribution of $250 to USBA, a nonprofit institution now incorporated in Louisiana. (Contributions are tax exempt.) Life members may vote and sanction tournaments.

Regular members, $10 annually, may also sanction tournaments and vote, as can club (in club name only) member, $10, and institution (in institution name only), $100. Under 23 members are $5.00 annually; they cannot vote nor sanction tournaments. All memberships receive all USBA publications.

Membership in USBA is required to participate in any USBA sanctioned tournament.

One extremely useful USBA publication is partially reprinted in the following pages. It lists, by zip code, clubs and contact persons in U.S. badminton. The original publication includes telephone numbers of these persons. Members may obtain the publication free; nonmembers pay $1.

INTERNATIONAL BADMINTON FEDERATION AND WORLD BADMINTON FEDERATION

The International Badminton Federation (IBF) and the World Badminton Federation (WBF) govern the sport internationally. USBA joined the IBF in 1938. Efforts are being made to unify these two organizations.

World Badminton, is the official quarterly periodical of the International Badminton Federation. It contains news, notes and reports from all over the world. To subscribe, write

> The Editor
> *World Badminton*
> Box 1272
> Moreton, N. B., Canada

Subscription price is only $5.

TOURNAMENTS

Many indoor tournaments are available to those who like competition. Information regarding location, chairmen, events, etc., can be found in *Badminton USA*. There are club, state, regional, intercollegiate and national championships for seniors, men, women and juniors in singles, doubles and mixed doubles events.

Professionalism in badminton is on a moderate scale, limited mainly to teaching professionals. More recently, commercialism has entered the picture with the advent of open badminton as of June 1979 approved by the International Badminton Federation. Prize money is being offered by the sponsors of tournaments, usually the equipment manufacturers.

The All England Championships is the oldest and most famous tournament in the world. It was first held in 1899 and attracts entries from many countries. Denmark, England, Indonesia, the United States, West Germany, Japan and Malaysia are the most active international participants.

The Thomas Cup is competed for triennally by men from countries that are affiliated with the IBF. Sir George Thomas donated this trophy for international competition among men's teams.

Results of the final rounds to date are as follows:

1948-49 Malaya defeated Denmark, 8-1
1951-52 Malaya defeated USA, 7-2
1954-55 Malaya defeated Denmark, 8-1
1957-58 Indonesia defeated Malaya, 6-3
1960-61 Indonesia defeated Thailand, 6-3
1963-64 Indonesia defeated Denmark, 5-4
1966-67 Malaysia defeated Indonesia, 6-3
1969-70 Indonesia defeated Malaysia, 6-2
1972-73 Indonesia defeated Denmark, 8-1
1975-76 Indonesia defeated Malaysia, 9-0
1978-79 Indonesia defeated Denmark, 9-0

Finalists in 1978-79 contest held in Jakarta, Indonesia, were: United States, New Zealand, Australia, Japan and Indonesia.

The Ladies International Badminton Championship for the Uber Cup is also held triennially. The team trophy was donated by one of England's greatest players, Mrs. H. S. (Betty) Uber.

Do you know who establishes the badminton rules for play in the United States? By whom is the sport governed for international matches?

Uber Cup

Results of the final rounds to date are as follows:

1956-57 United States defeated Denmark, 6-1
1959-60 United States defeated Denmark, 5-2

1962-63 United States defeated England, 4-3
1965-66 Japan defeated United States, 5-2
1968-69 Japan defeated Indonesia, 6-1
1971-72 Japan defeated Indonesia, 6-1
1974-75 Indonesia defeated Japan, 5-2
1977-78 Japan defeated Indonesia, 5-2

Finalists in 1977-78 contest held in Auckland, New Zealand: United States, New Zealand, Australia, Japan and Indonesia.

Current United States Champions are
1979 U.S. CLOSED WINNERS:

Men's Singles	Chris Kinard
Ladies' Singles	Pam Brady (formerly Stockton and Bristol)
Men's Doubles	Jim Poole and Mike Walker
Ladies' Doubles	Pam Brady and Judianne Kelly
Mixed Doubles	Mike Walker and Judianne Kelly

BADMINTON CAMP

For those who wish to get expert instruction and additional play, try the Connecticut Badminton Camp located at Miss Porter's School, Farmington, Connecticut. Held annually in August for one week, cost for boarding students is $225, and for day students, $110. During the morning students work on strokes, footwork and conditioning with the use of video tape instruction, evaluation, drills and practice.

In the afternoon there are coached games, lead-up games with additional teacher evaluation, strategy, video evaluation and instruction in court coverage. During the evening, students engage in informal play with other groups and coaches. In addition to badminton instruction, care and prevention of athletic injuries, suggested diet for athletes, practices and drills for large groups and tournament play are presented.

Those interested should direct their inquiries to

Ms. Rosemary McGuire
87 Lancaster Road
Bristol, Connecticut 06010
Telephone: (203) 582-9077

DO IT YOURSELF BADMINTON

For those people having trouble finding a place to play, there is now a portable badminton court available. It is made by Boltex at a cost of about $2,795.00. It can be laid in any gymnasium or high ceiling room. The overall size of the court is 49' x 23' in one piece which can be rolled up. It is lined and ready for play and includes the net, posts and dolly for handling. It can be installed on wood, asphalt, concrete, tile, clay or ice. This portable badminton court is available through Louisville Badminton Supply.

CLUBS AND CONTACT PERSONS IN THE UNITED STATES

Zip Code	Name and Address of Contact	Club Name
01760	Mara Nestle 12 Grove Street Natick, MA.	Maugus Club
01776	Vicki Edelman Sudbury, MA.	Lincoln-Sudbury Regional High School
01805	Dr. Carnela Virgilio Phys. Ed. Dept. State College at Westfield Westfield, MA.	State College at Westfield
01810	Jay Gottsfeld 4 Forbes Lane Andover, MA.	Phillips Academy
01830	Ms. Elizabeth Webber Bradford Junior College Bradford, MA.	Bradford Junior College
01890	Mary Francis Wright 30 Grove Street Winchester, MA.	Tufts University
01890	Rick Casey 2 Cutting Lane Winchester, MA.	Winchester
01915	Ms. Linda Anderson Phys. Ed. Dept. Endicott College Beverly, MA.	Endicott College
01945	Malcolm Heffelman 46 Pilgrim Road Marblehead, MA.	Tedesco
01945	Steve Wales 9 Columbia Road Marblehead, MA.	Gut 'N Feathers
01945	G. Steele Irons 47 Clifton Avenue Marblehead, MA.	Tedesco
01970	Ms. Maryellen McGee Phys. Ed. Dept. Salem State College Salem, MA.	Salem State College BC
01984	Andy Frederickson 44 Monument Street Wenham, MA.	Hamilton
02030	John Munroe 24 Haven Street Dover, MA.	Shady Hill

This list was compiled by the U.S.B.A.

Zip Code	Name and Address of Contact	Club Name
02090	Millie Maloof 48 Juniper Ridge Road Westwood, MA.	Westwood
02115	Ms. Evelyn Howard Northeastern University BBC 360 Huntington Avenue Boston, MA.	Boston-Bouve BC
02129	M.I.T. Badminton Club Dept. of Athletics, MIT Cambridge, MA.	M.I.T. Badminton Club
02146	Ms. Debbie Harrison 400 Heath Street Brookline, MA.	Pine Manor Junior College
02159	Ms. Edith Mold 777 Dedham Street Newton Centre, MA.	Mount Ida Junior College
02166	Mr. Crump, Mgr. 416 Stuart Street Boston, MA.	University Club
02173	Lynne Reem 351 Lincoln Street Lexington, MA.	Lexington
02181	John Charles Dept. of Phys. Ed. Wellesley, MA.	Wellesley College
02181	Mara Nestle 40 Abbott Road Wellesley, MA.	Maugus Club
02191	Park & Recreation Town Hall Needham, MA.	Needham
02193	Cathy Saravelas 24 Shady Hill Road Weston, MA.	Weston
02215	Agoes Judoprasetigo P.O. Box 385-Kenmore Station Boston, MA.	Boston University
02370	John Claude 210 Pond Street Rockland, MA.	Accord Pond Racquet Club
02402	James Lazour Director of Phys. Ed. 50 Summer Street Brockton, MA.	Brockton Public Schools
02714	Southeastern Mass. University North Dartmouth, MA.	

Zip Code	Name and Address of Contact	Club Name
02766	Ms. Hilda Mason Dept. of Phys. Ed. Norton, MA.	Wheaton College
02780	Mike Strojny 50 Oak Street Taunton, MA.	Taunton
03045	Ned Rivers 3 Pine Ridge Road Goffstown, NH.	Goffstown Badminton Association
03246	Lawrence Inglis Belknap Mt. Road Gilford, NH.	Gilford Badminton Club
03301	John Nelson 20 Pleasant Street Concord, NH.	N. H. Badminton Association
06013	Lewis Mills Dave Vibert Burlington, CT.	Har-Bur BC
06032	Miss Porter's School Rosemary McGuire Farmington, CT.	Matchpoint BC
06032	Irving Robbins S. Punch Ayer Farmington, CT.	Farmington BC
06035	Granby H. S. Roger Young Granby, CT.	Granby BC
06066	Vernon Middle S. W. J. Werkhoven Vernon, CT.	Vernon BC
06070	Henry James Mem. H. S. Gordon Bielecki Simsbury, CT.	Simsbury BC
06108	East Hartford Badminton Club Marie Schultz East Hartford, CT.	East Hartford BC
06105	St. Thomas Sem., Bloomf'd John P. Vann Greater Hartford, CT.	Greater Hartford BC
06111	Newington H. S. John Wallace Adolph Tenukus Newington, CT.	Newington BC
06340	Fitch H. S. Tony Neyaratally Groton, CT.	Groton BC

Zip Code	Name and Address of Contact	Club Name
06360	Norwich YMCA Al Riley Norwich, CT.	Norwich BC
064xx	Bethany Elementary Walt Berry Bethany, CT.	Bethany BC
06470	Middle School Frank Orosz Newton, CT.	Newtown BC
06477	Mary L. Tracy Tom McCarthy Orange, CT.	Orange BC
06830	Daycroft School Greenwich Ctry Day Steve Edson Greenwich, CT.	Greenwich BC
07043	Henry Sampers 101 Clarewill Avenue Upper Montclair, NJ.	Montclair BC
07834	Kirk A. Mellen 5 Basswood Drive Denville, NJ.	Mountain Lakes BC
07930	Mountain Lakes Rte #1 Box 221 Chester, NJ.	Mountain Lakes BC
07940	Sheene McClay 48 Dean Street Madison, NJ.	Mountain Lakes BC
11211	Pamela Domestico Brooklyn College Bedford Avenue & Avenue H Brooklyn, NY.	Brooklyn BC
07840	Abbie Ruthledge 400 Jefferson Street Hackettstown, NJ.	Centenary College Club
10021	Thomas Morrissey Buckley School Sports Complex Bldg. 210 East 74th Street Manhattan, NY.	Central Badminton Club
10021	Penn Davidson Buckley School 210 East 74th Street Manhattan, NY.	Chase Manhattan BC
10522	Scott Redfield Dobbs Ferry High School Dobbs Ferry, NY.	Dobbs Ferry BC

Zip Code	Name and Address of Contact	Club Name
11530	H. T. Chan Garden City Stratford Secondary School Garden City, L. I.	Garden City BC
10708	Anthony Mosca Bronxville Public School Pondfield Road and Midland Ave. Bronxville, NY.	Gramatan Hills BC
06830	Steve Edson Daycroft School and Greenwich Country Day School Greenwich, CT.	Greenwich BC
07039	Edith Young Mount Pleasant Jr. High School Mount Pleasant Avenue and Broadlawn Drive Livingston, NJ.	Livingston BC
11764	Pat McCarrick Miller Place High School Miller Place, NY.	Miller Place BC
07042	Henry Sampers, Jr. Hillside School Orange Road Montclair, NJ.	Montclair Badminton Club
07046	Bill Anderson Brier Cliff School Brier Cliff Road Mountain Lakes, NJ.	Mountain Lakes BC
10514	Art Murtha Horace Greeley High School Chappaqua, NY.	New Castle BC
07104	R. Swanson or M. Simon New Jersey Institute of Technology 323 High Street Newark, NJ.	N.J.I.T. Badminton Club
11375	Byron Igoe 4 Whitson Street Forest Hills, Queens	New York Athletic Club
11768	Theodore Bushell St. Paul's United Methodist Church 270 Main Street Northport, L. I.	Northport BC
11423	Tim Chao 88-33 188th Street Hollis, Queens	Queensborough Community College
07432	Leonard Pierce 125 Payne Avenue Midland Park, NJ.	Ridgewood BC

Zip Code	Name and Address of Contact	Club Name
10013	Joseph Morello St. Luke's Chapel Hudson and Grove Streets New York, NY.	St. Luke's BC
10028	Mrs. E. Bramwell 1225 Park Avenue New York, NY.	The BC of the City of New York
10017	Mrs. Burtis Frankenburg Church of the Covenant 310 East 42nd Street New York, NY.	Tudor City BC
10022	Sylvester Wong East Side International Community House 931 First Avenue New York, NY.	United Nations BC
10003	Gramercy Badminton Club 27 East 19th Street New York, NY.	Gramercy BC
10032	Badminton Players Club 3E 100 Haven Avenue New York, NY.	Badminton Players Club
10032	Dr. Rajiv Chandra 3E, 100 Haven Avenue New York, NY.	Metropolitan Badminton Association
11973	John Binnington Research Library Brookhaven National Laboratory Upton, NY.	BNL BC
13662	Sarah Jackson 39 Prospect Avenue Massena, NY.	Massena BC
16933	David J. Darby 214 Belknap Mansfield St. Col. Mansfield, PA.	Mansfield BC
13088	Carolyn Gressani 4989 Hopkins Road Liverpool, NY.	Meadows Racquet Club
17042	Harvey Snavely 2104 Water Street Lebanon, PA.	Lebanon BC
19104	Bob Mathews University of PA Philadelphia, PA.	University of PA. BC
19046	Jack Vaniver 1311 Fairacres Road Rydal, PA.	Wissahickon BC

Zip Code	Name and Address of Contact	Club Name
19119	Jack Vaniver Manheim & Morris Streets Philadelphia, PA.	Germantown Cricket Club
19122	Kaye Hart Athletic Director College of HPERD Philadelphia, PA.	Temple University Club
19128	John & Pat Cornell 225 Port Royal Avenue Philadelphia, PA.	Wissahickon BC
20016	Clay Norment 5500 Albemarle Street Washington, D. C.	BC of the District of Columbia
20037	Dr. Jim Breen George Washington University "K" Bldg. 23rd St. N.W. Washington, DC.	Washington, DC. Badminton Club
21204	Lynn Kuss 212-C Donnybrook Lane Towson, MD.	Homeland BC
21204	Vic Block 336 Stevenson Lane Baltimore, MD.	Homeland BC
23185	Badminton Coach Adair Gym College of William & Mary Williamsburg, VA.	College of William & Mary
30136	Buzz McGriff Athletic Club Drive Duluth, GA.	Atlanta Athletic Club BC
33145	Easter H. Smith 2312 S. W. 16 Terr. Miami, FL.	Miami BC
38118	Karen McDaniel 5057 Teal Memphis, TN.	Memphis BC
38138	W. T. McDaniel 5833 Vassar Street Memphis, TN.	Memphis BC
44022	Herb Wainer 30 Farmcote Drive Moreland Hills, OH.	Shaker Badminton Club
17604	Ross H. Sachs Athletic Office Lancaster, PA.	Franklin & Marshall BC

Zip Code	Name and Address of Contact	Club Name
44124	Susan Portmann 30599 Summit Lane Pepper Pike, OH.	Shaker BC
45371	John Obara 4714 East S. R. 571 & Obara Rd. Tipp City, OH.	Private—Obara
45701	Steve Abbott Box 159 GAM Ohio University Athens, OH.	Ohio Univ. BC
47304	Ms. Pat Brown 4612 N. Hereford Muncie, IN.	Muncie BC
48013	William Straith 1815 E. Tahquamenon Ct. Bloomfield Hills, MI.	Birmingham BC
48024	Hans Rogind 28925 Millbrook Road Farmington, MI.	Birmingham BC
48124	Lee Holmes 2010 Hollywood Dearborn, MI.	Westwood BC
48230	John Wood 1129 Nottingham Grosse Pte. Park, MI.	Grosse Pte. BC
48473	Gloria Eli 6303 Linden Road Swartz Creek, MI.	Flint BC
48507	Lynn Stockton 631 E. Atherton Flint, MI.	Mott BC
48507	Cleon McLaughlin 1726 Lynbrook Flint, MI.	Flint BC
48824	Janice Hrapsky Michigan State University East Lansing, MI.	MSU Badminton Club
49078	Harry G. Orr 1868 Jefferson Road Otsego, MI.	Kalamazoo BC
53186	Bill Adams 805 Westacone Avenue Waukesha, WI.	Univ. of Wisconsin BC
53202	Richard Wisnewski 756 No. Broadway Waukesha, WI.	Milwaukee Athletic Club

Zip Code	Name and Address of Contact	Club Name
53202	Bill Croft Walter Whitman Jr. High Wauwautosa, WI.	
53711	Carl Norton 6001 Piping Rock Road Madison, WI.	Madison Badminton Association
54601	Martie Stephens Wittich Hall LaCrosse, WI.	University Team, LaCrosse
54911	Walter Wieckert 43 S. Meadows Drive Appleton, WI.	Appleton Badminton Club
55402	Hal Raether (Ath. Dir.) 615 2nd Avenue So. Minneapolis, MN.	Minneapolis Athletic Club
60035	Dave Ramsay 442 Central Avenue, Apt. #3 Highland Park, IL.	
60050	Al Saxild 722 W. Rt. 120 McHenry, IL.	Grayslake Badminton Club
60093	Mike Zeddies 330 W. Frontage Road Northfield, IL.	Skokie Badminton Club
60160	William Richrach Walther Lutheran High School 9th Ave. and Superior Melrose Park, IL.	Chicago Badminton
60202	Robert Crown Center 1701 Main Street Evanston, IL.	
60201	Gary Silkaitis 1802 Maple Avenue Evanston, IL.	Evanston Badminton Club
60201	Tom Davey 2031 Pratt Court Evanston, IL.	Evanston Badminton Club
60202	Irv Finston 1804 Keeney Evanston, IL.	Evanston Badminton Club
60534	William Richrach Zion Lutheran 7930 Ogden Avenue Lyons, IL.	Chicago Badminton
60546	Margaret Werle 208 Blockbank Road Riverside, IL.	Chicago Badminton

Zip Code	Name and Address of Contact	Club Name
60632	Harold Deeman 2902 W. 39 PL Chicago, IL.	McKinley Park BC
61455	Donna Phillips Brophy Hall Western Illinois Univ.	
63122	Jim McQuie 756 Craig Drive Kirkwood, MO.	Beaumont Badminton Club
63122	Harold Thomas 3 Berrywood Drive Glendale, MO.	St. Louis Club
63122	Dick Witte 11959 Claychester Des Peres, MO.	St. Louis Club
68005	Len Williams 101 Caldor Drive Bellevue, NE.	Top Flight Badminton Club
68046	Raymond Scott 406 Circle Street Papillion, NE.	Top Flight Badminton Club
68046	John Frady R.R. #1 Omaha, NE.	Top Flight Badminton Club
68123	Col. Sheldon Lustig 3319 Coffey Avenue Omaha, NE.	Top Flight Badminton Club
70112	Taylor Caffery 1023 FNBC Building New Orleans, LA.	New Orleans Badminton Club
71104	Tom Carmody 1090 E. Kings Highway Shreveport, LA.	Shreveport Badminton Club
74601	Bob Chance 1000 S. Pine Ponca City, OK.	Conoco Badminton Club
75229	Felix Watson 2600 Northaven Dallas, TX.	Dallas Badminton Club
76703	Dutch Schroeder c/o Baylor Physical Edu. Dept. Waco, TX.	Baylor Badminton Club
77089	J. Terry Wilson 9835 Sageaspen Houston, TX.	Houston Badminton Club
77089	J. Terry Wilson 9835 Sageaspen Houston, TX.	YMCA Badminton Club

Zip Code	Name and Address of Contact	Club Name
77096	David Pollard 5726 Portal Drive Houston, TX.	Houston Badminton Club
78704	Frank Ray 1401 S. Congress Austin, TX.	Univ. of Texas BC
80203	Edmond E. Zimmerman 846 Broadway Denver, CO.	Mile High Badminton Club
88001	Harry Holguin New Mexico State Univ. Box 3M % Degler Las Cruces, NM.	Mesilla Valley BC
90066	Jo Kidd Recreation Department Santa Monica College 1900 Pico Blvd. Santa Monica, CA.	Santa Monica College "Weekend Co-Rec."
90230	L. A. Valley Badm. Club 11217 Washington Place #4 Culver City, CA.	L. A. Valley Badm. Club
90266	Wes Schoppe 657 25th Street Manhattan Beach, CA.	Manhattan Beach BC
90622	Duane Shelstad 421 3rd Street Manhattan Beach, CA.	Manhattan Beach BC
90803	Henry Saraye 2334 Broadway Long Beach, CA.	Long Beach BC
91011	Lois Alston 5359 Godbey Drive La Canada, CA.	Pasadena Badminton Club
91356	Cassandra Salapatas 18152 Rosita Street Tarzana, CA.	Valley Badminton Club
92122	San Diego Badminton Club 6135 Syracuse Lane San Diego, CA.	San Diego Badminton Club
92708	John Fleitz 17066 New Hope Street Fountain Valley, CA.	Los Caballeras Racquet
94080	Dick Ng 3945 Haussman So. San Francisco, CA.	
94544	Jerry Eichelberger 24885 Broadmore Avenue Hayward, CA.	Oakland Badminton Club

Zip Code	Name and Address of Contact	Club Name
94556	George Frederickson 141 Fernwood Drive Moraga, CA.	
94590	Ozzie Hilton 1415 Illinois Street P.O. Box 4157 Vallejo, CA.	
94590	Jim Jordan 124 Interstate 80 Vallejo, CA.	Pterodactyl Badminton Club
95138	David Yonemoto 474 Piercy Road San Jose, CA.	Peninsula Badminton Club
95620	Lillian R. Butterfield 545 Peterson Lane Dixon, CA.	U. C. Davis Badminton Team
95821	James Bosco 3117 Delwood Way Sacramento, CA.	CSUS Badminton Club
96701	Louis Ach 98-715 IHO Place, Apt. 704 AIEA, HI.	Honolulu Badminton Club
96720	Richard Nagano 2076 Kinook Street Hilo, HI.	Hilo Badminton Club
97023	John Rowley P.O. Box 247, 318 Cliff Lane Estacada, OR.	Estacada Badminton Club
97207	Louise Cicrich 1849 S.W. Salmon Street Portland, OR.	Multnomah Athletic
92805	Long Beach Badminton Club 402 Winston Road Anaheim, CA. 92805	Long Beach Badminton Club
50318	C. J. Farr Des Moines Center Field House 18 to 809 So. 228th Des Moines, IA.	
98101	Joyce Chinnick Washington Athletic Club 1325 6th Ave. Seattle, WA.	
98106	Tennis World 7245 W. Marginal Way Seattle, WA.	

Zip Code	Name and Address of Contact	Club Name
98108	Athletic Dept. Tacoma Community College 5900 S. 12th Tacoma, WA.	
98122	Rupe Topp Seattle Tennis Club 922 McGilvra Blvd. Seattle, WA.	Seattle Tennis Club
98133	Don Jones 11616 Aurora N. Seattle, WA.	Gallery Tennis Club
98133	Dick Pierce Highline High School 225 So. 152nd So. Seattle, WA.	
98146	Jan Contento 1321 S.W. 102nd Seattle, WA.	
98155	Joyce Chinnick 16245 N.E. 24th Bellevue Seattle, WA.	
98155	Joyce Jones 18560 1st N.E. N. King Co. Seattle, WA.	
98188	Dick Pierce 4424 So. 189th So. King Co. Seattle, WA.	
98362	Hester Hill 915 So. Washington Street Port Angeles, WA.	Port Angeles BC

selected references

Books

ANNARINO, ANTHONY A. *Badminton Instruction Program.* Englewood Cliffs, N.J.: Prentice-Hall, 1973. $2.75.

BURRIS, BARBARA and OLSON, ARNE. *Badminton* (Sports Techniques Series). Chicago: Athletic Institute (805 Merchandise Mart Plaza), 1970. $1.95.

DAVIDSON, KEN and GUSTAVSON, LEA. *Winning Badminton.* New York: Ronald Press, 1964. $4.50.

DAVIS, PAT. *The Badminton Coach: A Manual for Coaches, Teachers, and Players.* New Rochelle, N.Y.: Sportshelf, 1976. $15.25.

HICKS, VIRGINIA. *The How to of Badminton From Player to Teacher.* Denton, Tx: Terrell Wheeler Printing, Inc., 1973.

JOHNSON, M. L. *Badminton.* Philadelphia: W. B. Saunders Co., 1974. $3.00.

POOLE, JAMES. *Badminton.* (Goodyear Physical Activities Series). Pacific Palisades, CA: Goodyear Publishing Co., 1973. $3.95.

ROGERS, WYNN. *Advanced Badminton.* (Physical Education Activities Series). Dubuque, IA: Wm. C. Brown Company Publishers, 2460 Kerper Blvd., 1970. $3.50 (approx.)

Magazines and Guides

Badminton Rules. Dayton Racquet Co., Arcanum, OH 45304. Free.

Badminton Rules. United States Badminton Association, P.O. Box 237, Swartz Creek, MI 48473. 50¢.

Badminton USA. Official Publication of the United States Badminton Association, P.O. Box 237, Swartz Creek, MI 48473.

Canadian Badminton Association Handbook. 75¢. Also *Level I Coaching Manual,* $2.50 and *Level II Coaching Manual,* $3.50. 333 River Road, Ottawa, Ontario, Canada.

IBF Handbook. International Badminton Federation. £1.50. 7 Hartlebury Way, Charleton Kings, Cheltenham Gloucestershire, GL52 6YB England.

Racquets Canada. 643 Yonge St., Toronto, Canada.

Selected Tennis and Badminton Articles. NAGWS-AAHPER, 1201 16th St., N.W., Washington, DC 20036.

Tennis-Badminton Guide. NAGWS-AAHPER, 1201 16th St., N.W., Washington, DC 20036.

World Badminton. United States Badminton Association, P.O. Box 237. Swartz Creek, MI. 48473.

Visual Aids

Advanced Badminton. Wynn Rogers. Aims Instructional Media Services, Inc., P.O. Box 1010, Hollywood, CA 90028.

Badminton Fundamentals. Aims Instructional Media Services, Inc., P.O. Box 1010, Hollywood, CA 90028.

Badminton Movies. Louisville Badminton Supply, 9411 Westport Road, Louisville, KY 40222.

Badminton Sound Films. AAHPER Educational Media Services, 1201 16th St., N.W., Washington, DC 20036.

Badminton Sound Super 8 Cassettes. 1974. AAHPER Educational Media Services, 1201 16th St., N.W. Washington, DC 20036.

Selected Highlights of the 1969 U.S. Open Amateur Championships. David Ogata, 3919 Alla Road, Los Angeles, CA 90066.

Selected Highlights of the 1973 U.S. Open Amateur Championships. Travelers Insurance Companies, 1 Tower Square, Hartford, CT 06115.

questions and answers

TRUE OR FALSE

1. The thumb is placed on the back bevel of the handle for the forehand grip.
   (p. 8)
2. The racket is held firmly in the palm of the hand. (p. 8)
3. Backpedaling is the skill of moving backwards, peculiar to the game of badminton. (p. 12)
4. A legal serve includes both the contact point and racket head being below the wrist. (pp. 13-14)
5. The serve is considered a defensive stroke because it is played underhand and must therefore be hit upwards. (p. 16)
6. The overhead and forehand strokes originate high above the head with the wrist cocked. (p. 18)
7. The trajectory of the attacking clear is lower than the defensive clear. (p. 19)
8. The dropshot must be deceptive since its flight is slow. (p. 21)
9. A smash played from the backcourt will have less downward angle than one played nearer the net. (p. 30)
10. With proper timing it is not necessary to use shoulder and arm strength to obtain power. (p. 32)
11. A drive may be played deep and fast or slower to midcourt, as well as crosscourt and down-the-line. (p. 24)
12. The backhand clear is one of the easiest strokes to play and perfect. (p. 34)
13. The half-smash has little value since it has less peed than a full smash. (p. 32)
14. The round-the-head shot is a forehand shot played above the left shoulder.
    (p. 34)
15. The driven serve is designed to push the receiver to the backcourt. (p. 36)
16. Net shots are played with the same wrist and shoulder action as other shots for proper deception. (p. 27)
17. Underhand shots are considered offensive shots because if deceptive they can keep the opponent from guessing their direction. (p. 33)

18. "Holding the shuttle" is a deceptive technique useful against a slow-moving player. (p. 37)

19. Repeated practice of each stroke separately tends to make a player lose the sense of game play. (p. 40)

20. Practicing or playing with a player of like ability produces maximum benefits. (p. 40)

21. Defensive play can be changed to offensive play depending on how well a stroke is executed and selected for use at the time. (p. 45)

22. Angle of return in badminton is relatively unimportant since the court is only twenty feet wide. (p. 45)

23. Crosscourt shots are best used when your opponent has not been drawn from the center position. (p. 46)

24. Receiving serve in a diagonal (forward and back) stance allows the receiver to best cover the area to either side of him. (p. 47)

25. In singles, the object is to move your opponent forward and back, using low serves, drives and dropshots. (p. 48)

26. The half-smash and dropshot are often used to change defense into attack. (p. 48)

27. A short clear should be returned with a smash or dropshot. (p. 39)

28. In singles, the forehand side of the court may be vulnerable due to extra effort made compensating for weakness on the backhand. (p. 46)

29. In doubles, teams should decide to play side-by-side or up-and-back without changing this formation during a point. (p. 50)

30. Offense and defense are determined by the angle of the flight of the shuttle. (p. 45)

31. The side-by-side formation lends itself best to attack. (p. 50)

32. The up-and-back formation is best attacked with halfcourt shots. (p. 51)

33. A high deep clear allows a team to assume the up-and-back positions. (p. 51)

34. A well played halfcourt shot should lead both opponents to believe it is his shot to return. (p. 51)

35. In mixed doubles, the woman should seldom make an attempt to return smashes and fast drives. (p. 53)

36. Except when there is a set-up, the net player in doubles uses many halfcourt and net shots. (p. 52)

37. There is a special formation to use in mixed doubles when the opposing man plays an overhead smash. (p. 54)

38. The woman in mixed doubles should play the shuttle deep to the corners. (p. 52)

39. In mixed doubles, the man should attempt to play most of the shots and direct them to the opposing woman. (p. 54)

40. A balk is a deceptive and delaying movement used as a means of gaining a point. (p. 55)

41. A carry is legal provided the flight of the shuttle is not drastically altered. (p. 56)

42. A flick shot refers to shots played with an overhead stroke to surprise an opponent. (p. 57)

43. A shuttle is "in play" when the serve crosses the net. (p. 57)

44. The serving side wins the point when a let is called. (p. 57)

45. The term "second service" means the team which did not serve first. (p. 58)

46. When setting, the player reaching the tied score first has the option of setting. (p. 58)

47. A shot played off the wood of the racket is legal. (p. 59)

48. The heavier the shuttle, the faster it flies. (p. 60)

49. A player losing the toss has no choices. (p. 61)

50. In a three-game doubles match, players change ends when one team scores eight points. (p. 62)

51. A doubles team may not change its order of service during the match. (p. 62)

52. It is considered poor sportsmanship to change the speed of the shuttle by bending the feathers. (p. 4)

53. A shuttlecock will have a slower flight at a high altitude and with low humidity. (p. 60)

54. Tournaments are played both indoors and outdoors at a sectional and national level. (p. 72)

COMPLETION

55. Identify the names of the following lines and areas of a badminton court.

1. _____
2. _____
3. _____
4. _____
5. _____
6. _____
7. _____
8. _____
9. _____
10. _____   (pp. 6-7)

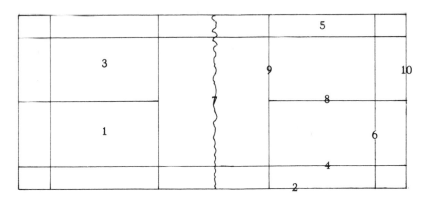

Complete the blanks:

56. Net heights _____   (pp. 6-7)

57. Shuttle weights _____   (pp. 6-7)

58. Minimum ceiling height _____   (pp. 6-7)

Give the required number of points for:

59. Ladies singles _____   (p. 2)

60. Mens singles _____   (p. 2)

61. Doubles _____   (p. 2)

62. Score set at 9 all _____   (p. 2)

63. Score set at 10 all _____   (p. 2)

64. Score set at 13 all _____   (p. 2)

65. Score set at 14 all _____   (p. 2)

66. On the court below draw and number the flight patterns for the following
    strokes:
    1. Defensive Clear
    2. Attacking Clear
    3. Overhead Dropshot
    4. Smash
    5. High Singles Serve
    6. Low Doubles Serve
    7. High Doubles Serve
    8. Drive
    9. Hairpin Net Shot
    10. Underhand Clear

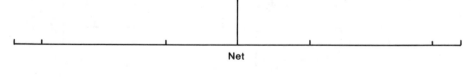

Net

Select one of the following letters to best answer the question.

A. point	E. second service
B. service over	F. legal
C. let	G. disqualification
D. fault	H. poor etiquette

67. A player attempting a serve, misses the shuttle completely.   (p. 62)

68. A smash played by the server hits the very outside of the line.   (p. 63)

69. After the serve a player inadvertently places one foot outside the boundary lines
    to play the shuttle.   (p. 63)

70. In singles, the server's score is seven and he serves from the right court and wins the rally. (p. 63)

71. Neither the linesman nor the umpire can make a decision when the serving side served a shuttle which fell very close to the short service line. (p. 63)

72. The server contacts the shuttle below the waist and the racket head below the hand. (p. 63)

73. The server in singles takes a step before the shuttle is contacted. (p. 64)

74. The receiver unsuccessfully returns a serve he claims was served before he was ready. (p. 64)

75. In double, the receiver receives serve in the wrong court and wins the rally. (p. 64)

76. In doubles, a player receives serve twice in succession and the serving side wins both rallies. (p. 64)

77. The receiver's partner is able to return a serve his partner cannot reach and scores a winner. (p. 64)

78. The shuttle passes between the net and net post and falls into the proper court. (p. 64)

79. A player contacts the shuttle on his side but the racket head carries over the net. (p. 64)

80. A player touches the net on the follow through of a smash after the shuttle hit the floor. (p. 64)

81. The server hits an opponent with a shuttle which is going out. (p. 65)

82. The net player is able to return a smash by ducking below the net and putting his racket up to intercept the shuttle. (p. 65)

83. In mixed doubles, the server places himself behind his partner in order to hide the shuttle from the receiver. (p. 65)

84. A player consults his coach between games. (p. 66)

85. A player calls no shot or fault whenever it occurs during play. (p. 66)

86. In doubles, with the score 8-7, the first server serves and the serve hits the top of the net and goes into the correct court. (p. 64)

ANSWERS TO EVALUATION QUESTIONS

Page | Answer and Page Reference

10   The thumb is placed flat against the back bevel in order to give greater support for a deep hit. (p. 10)

12   It is more important not to be moving when the opponent hits the shuttle. (p. 12)

14   No answer.

20   The defensive clear diagonally cross court from corner to corner requires the most power. (pp. 18-19)

22   A good dropshot deceives the opponent and falls as far from center court as possible. (pp. 20-21)

27   The feet, body, and upper arm are simply used for reaching rather than for stroking net shots. (p. 27)

Page   Answer and Page Reference

36   The half-smash requires less effort than the smash and the recovery is easier.
          The use of the backhand stroke permits the feet and body to remain nearer
          center court.   (pp. 32-36)

38   The height of the shuttle when it is to be stroked is the first determinant of
          which stroke or strokes are possible. A smash from close to the net depends al-
          most solely on wrist snap for its force whereas the body weight is thrown into
          a smash from a deeper court position.   (pp. 30-32, 39)

50   The smash, half-smash, drop shot or attacking clear are good returns. (p. 48)

51   The sides of the court and the area just behind the net player are most vul-
          nerable in the up-and-back formation. For the side-by-side formation, base-
          line, front court, and center line areas are less easily defended.   (pp. 50-51)

54   When defending against the possibility of a crosscourt smash, the woman
          should move a few feet backward.   (p. 54)

59   See definitions on pages indicated.   (pp. 56-59)

62   The team first reaching the score of 13 has the option of setting. At 14-all,
          the setting option is available if not taken at 13-all. Again, the first team
          to reach the score makes the decision.   (p. 62)

72   The United States Badminton Association sets the rules for this country.
          The International and World Badminton Federations govern international
          play.   (pp. 70-71)

KNOWLEDGE TEST ANSWER KEY

True or False

1. F	12. F	23. F	34. T	45. F
2. F	13. F	24. F	35. T	46. T
3. F	14. T	25. F	36. T	47. T
4. T	15. F	26. T	37. T	48. T
5. T	16. F	27. T	38. F	49. F
6. F	17. F	28. T	39. F	50. T
7. T	18. F	29. F	40. F	51. F
8. T	19. F	30. T	41. F	52. T
9. T	20. T	31. F	42. F	53. F
10. F	21. T	32. T	43. F	54. F
11. T	22. F	33. F	44. F	

Completion

55. 1. Right Service Court
     2. Side Boundary Line (doubles)
     3. Left Service Court
     4. Side Boundary Line (singles)
     5. Alley
     6. Long Service Line for Doubles
     7. Net
     8. Center Line
     9. Short Service Line
    10. Back Boundary Line and Long Service Line for Singles
56. 5' center, 5'1" posts
57. 73-85 grains
58. 25' above center of net
59. 11 points
60. 15 points

61. 15 points
62. 3 points
63. 2 points
64. 5 points
65. 3 points
66.

NET

67. C   77. A or D
68. A   78. D
69. F   79. F
70. B   80. F
71. C   81. A
72. F   82. D
73. B or D   83. D
74. A   84. G
75. C   85. H
76. A   86. F

index